STAR WARS

WORKBOOKS

3RD GRADE MATH

FOR AGES 8–9

BY THE EDITORS OF BRAIN QUEST
CONSULTING EDITOR: BRYAN HOLLEY

WORKMAN PUBLISHING
NEW YORK

BRAIN QUEST and WORKMAN are registered trademarks of Workman Publishing Co., Inc.

Library of Congress Cataloging-in-Publication Data is available.

ISBN 978-0-7611-8935-0

Workbook series designer Raquel Jaramillo
Designers Tim Hall, Abby Dening
Writers Claire Piddock, Megan Butler
Editors Nathalie Le Du, Olivia Swomley, Zoe Maffitt
Production Editor Jessica Rozler
Production Manager Julie Primavera

Workman books are available at special discounts when purchased in bulk for premiums and sales promotions as well as for fund-raising or educational use. Special editions or book excerpts can also be created to specification. For details, contact the Special Sales Director at the address below, or send an email to specialmarkets@workman.com.

Workman Publishing Co., Inc.
225 Varick Street
New York, NY 10014-4381

workman.com
starwars.com
starwarsworkbooks.com

Printed in the United States of America

First printing November 2017

10 9 8 7 6 5 4 3 2 1

STAR WARS

WORKBOOKS

This workbook belongs to:

_____

About How Many?

Plot the number of droids on the number line. Then round to the nearest hundred to estimate the number of droids.

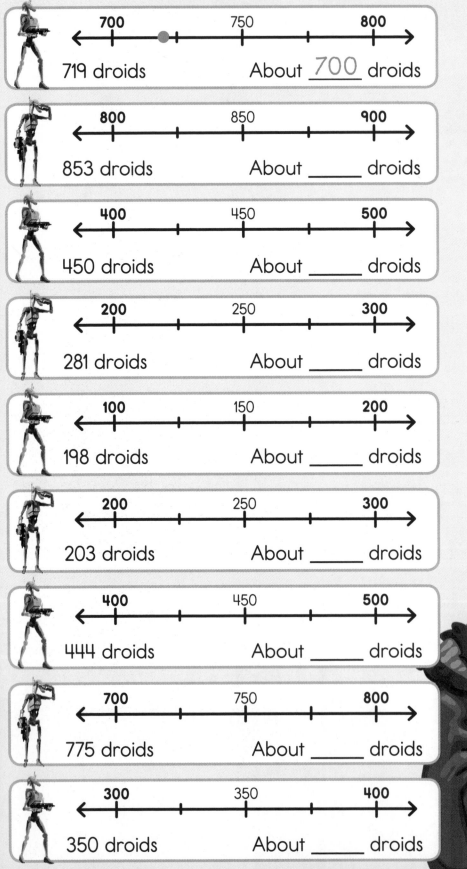

700   750   800

719 droids   About <u>700</u> droids

800   850   900

853 droids   About _____ droids

400   450   500

450 droids   About _____ droids

200   250   300

281 droids   About _____ droids

100   150   200

198 droids   About _____ droids

200   250   300

203 droids   About _____ droids

400   450   500

444 droids   About _____ droids

700   750   800

775 droids   About _____ droids

300   350   400

350 droids   About _____ droids

50 or greater, round up.
49 or less, round down.

Plot the number of droids on the number line.
Then round to the nearest ten to estimate the
number of droids.

5 or greater,
round up.
4 or less,
round down.

50   55   60

52 droids   About __50__ droids

10   15   20

17 droids   About _____ droids

20   25   30

25 droids   About _____ droids

680   685   690

682 droids   About _____ droids

210   215   220

211 droids   About _____ droids

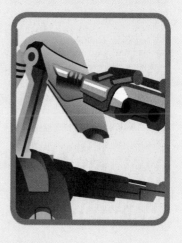

630   635   640

636 droids   About _____ droids

170   175   180

175 droids   About _____ droids

Playing Patterns

Imagine that you are Finn. Start at 1. Add 4. Circle the squares that show Finn's **addition pattern** in blue.

Imagine that Finn is playing against Kylo Ren. Kylo Ren starts at 9 and adds 5. Circle the squares that show his addition pattern in red.

(1)	2	3	4	(5)	6	7	8	(9)	10
11	12	13	(14)	15	16	17	18	19	20
21	22	23	24	25	26	27	28	29	30
31	32	33	34	35	36	37	38	39	40
41	42	43	44	45	46	47	48	49	50
51	52	53	54	55	56	57	58	59	60
61	62	63	64	65	66	67	68	69	70
71	72	73	74	75	76	77	78	79	80
81	82	83	84	85	86	87	88	89	90
91	92	93	94	95	96	97	98	99	100

Finn and Kylo Ren battle when they are on the same square.
Write the numbers of the squares where they battle.

_____

Even numbers end in 0, 2, 4, 6, or 8.
Odd numbers end in 1, 3, 5, 7, or 9.

Add the number in the top row to the number in the left column to fill in the missing sum in each shaded square.

+	0	1	2	3	4	5	6	7	8	9
0	0	1	2	3	4	5	6	7	8	9
1	1	2	3	4	5	6	7	8	9	10
2	2	3	4	5	6	7	8	9	10	11
3	3	4	5	6	7	8	9	10	11	12
4	4	5	6	7		9	10	1	12	13
5	5	6	7	8	9	10	11	12	13	14
6	6	7	8	9		11	12	13	14	15
7	7	8		10		12		14		16
8	8	9	10	1		13	14	15	16	17
9	9	10	11	12	13	14	15	16	17	18

Fill in the blanks to complete each sentence.

Finn lands on the blue squares, which are all __even__ numbers.

The sum of an even number and even number is an _____ number.

Kylo Ren lands on the red squares, which are all _____ numbers.

The sum of an odd and an even number is an _____ number.

The Ewoks Are Multiplying!

When you **multiply**, you find the total of equal groups.

2 equal groups of 4 Ewoks equals 8 Ewoks.

2 x 4 = 8 Ewoks

Fill in the blanks to complete each multiplication sentence.

3 x ___ = ____ Ewoks

___ x 4 = ____ Ewoks

4 x ___ = ____ Ewoks

An **array** is a group of objects arranged in equal rows and equal columns. When you multiply, you repeatedly add groups or rows.

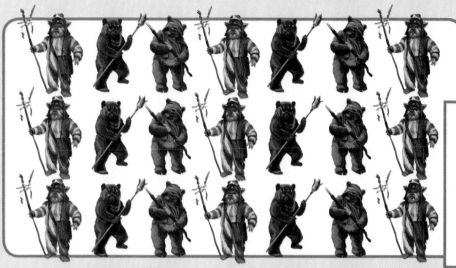

3 rows of 7 Ewoks equals 21 Ewoks.

7 + 7 + 7 = 21 Ewoks

3 x 7 = 21 Ewoks

Look at the arrays. Fill in the blanks to complete each addition and multiplication sentence.

___ + ___ = 18 Ewoks

2 x ___ = ___ Ewoks

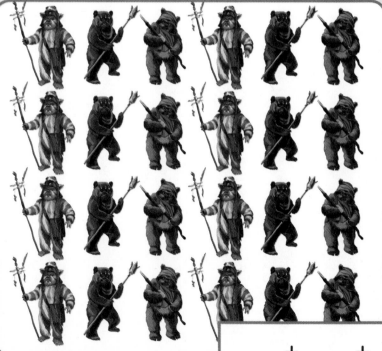

___ + ___ + ___ + ___ = ___ Ewoks

___ x ___ = ___ Ewoks

Break the Code

Multiply to find the **product**.
Use the products to decode the answer to the question.

4 x 3 = _____ **Y**

8 x 5 = _____ **O**

6 x 5 = _____ **N**

3 x 9 = _____ **K**

4 x 9 = _____ **R**

7 x 6 = _____ **E**

9 x 7 = _____ **L**

8 x 7 = _____ **B**

9 x 5 = _____ **A**

Question:

Which commander of the First Order is also Han and Leia's son?

Answer:

___ ___ ___ ___   ___ ___ ___
27   12   63   40   36   42   30

Speedy Shortcut

Use **math facts** and **place value** to multiply the BB-8s by tens.

3 x 40 = 3 groups of 4 tens

Shortcut!
Use the multiplication fact **3 x 4 = 12**. Then write a **0** at the end.

4 tens + 4 tens + 4 tens = 12 tens
40 + 40 + 40 = 120

7 x 20 = 7 groups of 2 tens

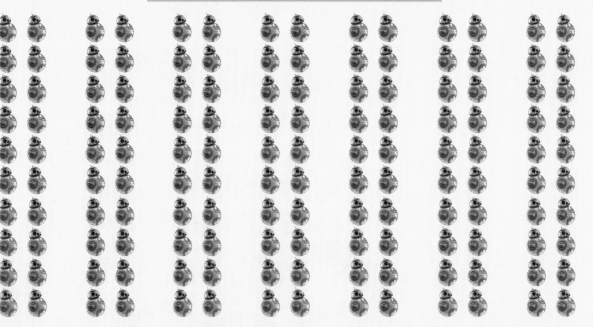

2 tens + 2 tens + 2 tens + 2 tens + 2 tens + 2 tens + 2 tens = _____ tens

20 + 20 + 20 + 20 + 20 + 20 + = _____

Use the shortcut to find each product.

3 x 30 = 3 x 3 tens =

_____ tens = _____

5 x 70 = 5 x 7 tens =

_____ tens = _____

9 x 80 = 9 x 8 tens =

_____ tens = _____

4 x 50 = 4 x 5 tens =

_____ tens = _____

6 x 40 = 6 x 4 tens =

_____ tens = _____

Stormtroopers

The **commutative property** says that you can multiply in any order.

4 teams of 3 troopers	3 teams of 4 troopers
$4 \times 3 = 12$	$3 \times 4 = 12$

4 x 3	=	3 x 4

Use the commutative property to complete each math fact.

$5 \times 7 = \underline{7} \times \underline{5}$

$3 \times 7 = \underline{} \times \underline{}$

$2 \times 9 = \underline{} \times \underline{}$

$3 \times 8 = \underline{} \times \underline{}$

$4 \times 9 = \underline{} \times \underline{}$

$5 \times 8 = \underline{} \times \underline{}$

$5 \times 6 = \underline{} \times \underline{}$

$4 \times 8 = \underline{} \times \underline{}$

Grouping with TIE Fighters

The **associative property** says that when you multiply more than two numbers, you can group the factors in different ways.

Multiply **3 x 2 x 4**.

(3 x 2) x 4   or   3 x (2 x 4)

6 x 4   or   3 x 8

24   or   24

You can multiply either way.
The product is the same.

Draw **parentheses ( )** to show which factors you multiply first. Then find the products.

5 x 2 x 2

$(5 \times 2) \times 2$ or $5 \times (2 \times 2)$

10 x 2   or   5 x 4

_20_   or   _20_

3 x 2 x 2

3 x 2 x 2   or   3 x 2 x 2

6 x 2   or   3 x 4

____   or   ____

4 x 2 x 5

4 x 2 x 5 or 4 x 2 x 5

8 x 5 or 4 x 10

_____ or _____

2 x 6 x 2

2 x 6 x 2 or 2 x 6 x 2

12 x 2 or 2 x 12

_____ or _____

2 x 3 x 4

2 x 3 x 4 or 2 x 3 x 4

6 x 4 or 2 x 12

_____ or _____

5 x 2 x 3

5 x 2 x 3 or 5 x 2 x 3

10 x 3 or 5 x 6

_____ or _____

4 x 2 x 6

4 x 2 x 6 or 4 x 2 x 6

8 x 6 or 4 x 12

_____ or _____

Fighter Formations

You can break apart a factor in a multiplication problem to make two easier multiplication problems. Then you find the sum.

These X-wing fighters are in **4 x 9** formation.

4 x 9 = ?

If you break apart the fighters with a green line, you can make two formations.

4 x 9 = 4 x (4 + 5)
4 x 9 = (4 x 4) + (4 x 5)
4 x 9 = __16__ + __20__
4 x 9 = __36__

You can break apart the formation in a different way. Fill in the blanks.

4 x 9 = 4 x (2 + 7)
4 x 9 = (4 x 2) + (4 x 7)
4 x 9 = ____ + ____
4 x 9 = ____

Draw a line to show how to break apart the formation according to the problems in the boxes. Then fill in the blanks.

$4 \times 9 = 4 \times (6 + 3)$

$4 \times 9 = (4 \times \underline{\quad}) + (4 \times \underline{\quad})$

$4 \times 9 = \underline{\quad} + \underline{\quad}$

$4 \times 9 = \underline{\quad}$

$3 \times 10 = 3 \times (5 + 5)$

$3 \times 10 = (3 \times \underline{\quad}) + (3 \times \underline{\quad})$

$3 \times 10 = \underline{\quad} + \underline{\quad}$

$3 \times 10 = \underline{\quad}$

$3 \times 10 = 3 \times (3 + 7)$

$3 \times 10 = (3 \times \underline{\quad}) + (3 \times \underline{\quad})$

$3 \times 10 = \underline{\quad} + \underline{\quad}$

$3 \times 10 = \underline{\quad}$

Droid Division

When you **divide**, you split a total number of objects into smaller, equal groups.

Draw circles around the droids to make equal groups and then fill in the blanks.

Make **three** equal groups.

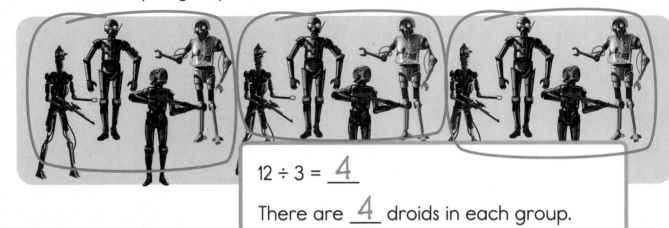

$12 ÷ 3 =$ __4__

There are __4__ droids in each group.

Make **two** equal groups.

$16 ÷ 2 =$ ____

There are ____ droids in each group.

Make **five** equal groups.

$15 ÷ 5 =$ ____

There are ____ droids in each group.

Put **seven** droids in each group.

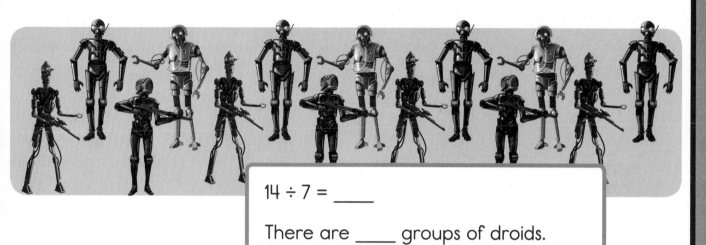

14 ÷ 7 = _____

There are _____ groups of droids.

Put **two** droids in each group.

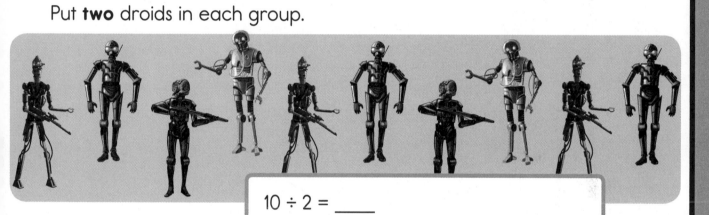

10 ÷ 2 = _____

There are _____ groups of droids.

Put **three** droids in each group.

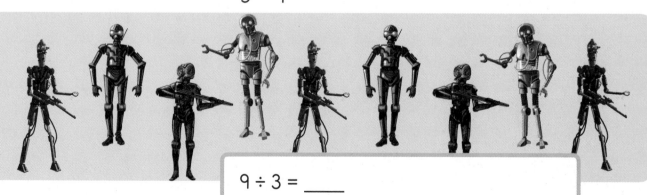

9 ÷ 3 = _____

There are _____ groups of droids.

Forceful Formations

An **array** shows how multiplication and division are related fact families.

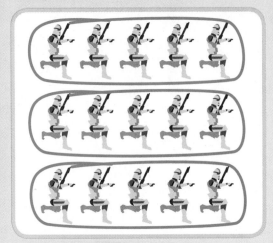

This array of clone troopers shows 3 groups of 5.

3 x 5 = 15

The same array also shows 15 clone troopers divided into equal groups (rows) of 5. There are 3 rows.

15 ÷ 5 = 3

This array of clone troopers shows 5 groups of 3.

5 x 3 = 15

The same array also shows 15 clone troopers divided into equal groups (columns) of 3. There are 5 columns.

15 ÷ 3 = 5

Identify the related facts that the array shows. Circle the groups. Then complete the equations.

3 x _____ = _____

18 ÷ _____ = 3

6 x _____ = _____

18 ÷ _____ = 6

_____ x _____ = 28

28 ÷ _____ = _____

_____ x _____ = 28

28 ÷ _____ = _____

_____ x _____ = 16

16 ÷ _____ = _____

_____ x _____ = 16

16 ÷ _____ = _____

Draw an array to show 2 groups of 9 clone troopers and
9 groups of 2 clone troopers. Write the related fact families.

_____ x _____ = _____

_____ ÷ _____ = _____

_____ x _____ = _____

_____ ÷ _____ = _____

Creature Word Problems

Read each word problem. Write an equation using n for the unknown number. Then solve. (Draw arrays if you need to.)

Reeks have **3** horns on their heads. How many horns do **5** reeks have in all?

<u> 5 x 3 = *n* </u>   <u> 15 </u> horns

A Kowakian monkey-lizard has **3** claws on each hand and foot. How many claws will the animal's **4** hands and feet have in all?

_____ _____ claws

Each rancor has **4** strong arms and legs. If Anakin sees **24** arms and legs attacking, how many rancors are there?

_____ _____ rancors

Each gargoyle has **2** glowing eyes. If you see **18** eyes, how many gargoyles are hiding?

_____ ____ gargoyles

Banthas have **4** legs and **2** horns. How many legs will **8** banthas have?

_____ ____ legs

How many horns will **6** banthas have?

_____ ____ horns

Gamorreans have **2** horns and **4** fangs. How many horns will **4** Gamorreans have?

_____ ____ horns

How many fangs will **3** Gamorreans have?

_____ ____ fangs

Tied-Up Trouble

Multiplication and division fact families can help you find a **quotient** (the answer to a division problem). You can divide by using multiplication facts.

| $3 \times 9 = 27$ | so | $27 \div 9 = 3$ | | $9 \times 3 = 27$ | so | $27 \div 3 = 9$ |

Tie up and bring down the AT-AT by drawing lines to match the related multiplication and division facts.

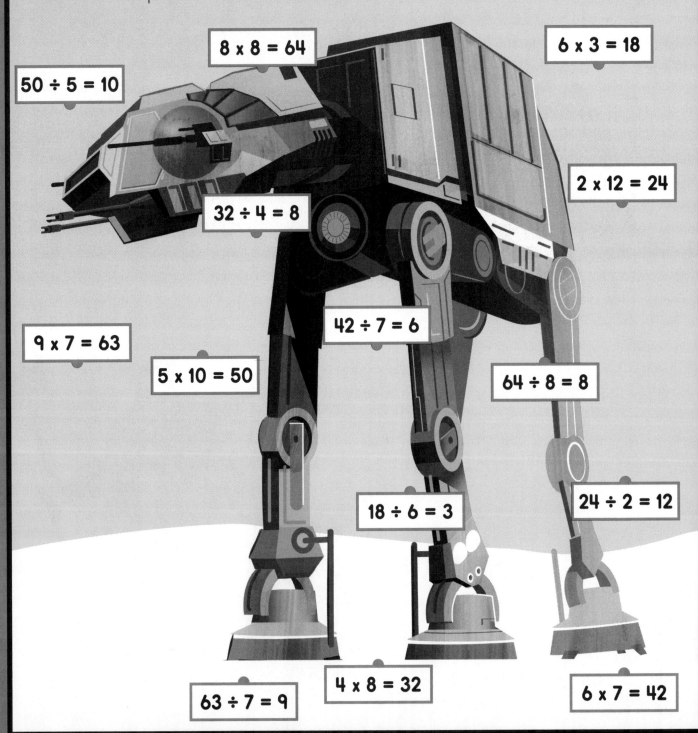

$8 \times 8 = 64$

$6 \times 3 = 18$

$50 \div 5 = 10$

$2 \times 12 = 24$

$32 \div 4 = 8$

$42 \div 7 = 6$

$9 \times 7 = 63$

$5 \times 10 = 50$

$64 \div 8 = 8$

$24 \div 2 = 12$

$18 \div 6 = 3$

$4 \times 8 = 32$

$63 \div 7 = 9$

$6 \times 7 = 42$

Tie up and bring down the AT-AT by drawing lines to match the related multiplication and division facts. Then fill in the products or quotients.

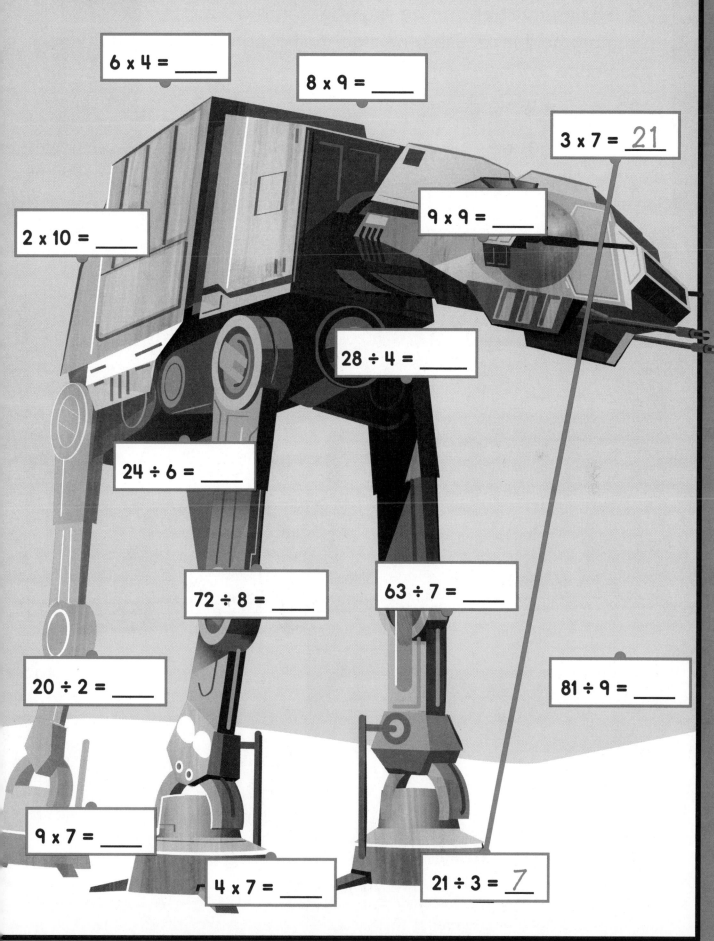

6 x 4 = _____

8 x 9 = _____

3 x 7 = _21_

2 x 10 = _____

9 x 9 = _____

28 ÷ 4 = _____

24 ÷ 6 = _____

72 ÷ 8 = _____

63 ÷ 7 = _____

20 ÷ 2 = _____

81 ÷ 9 = _____

9 x 7 = _____

4 x 7 = _____

21 ÷ 3 = _7_

Dagobah Division

A **missing number** can be anywhere in a division number sentence. Use a related multiplication sentence to find the missing number.

$20 \div \underline{\hphantom{00}} = 4$

$4 \times \underline{\hphantom{00}} = 20$

$4 \times 5 = 20$, so $20 \div \underline{5} = 4$

$\underline{30} \div 3 = 10$

$40 \div \underline{\hphantom{00}} = 5$

$\underline{\hphantom{00}} \div 6 = 3$

$\underline{\hphantom{00}} \div 7 = 7$

$15 \div \underline{\hphantom{00}} = 3$

$81 \div \underline{\hphantom{00}} = 9$

A missing number can be **anywhere** in a multiplication number sentence. Use a related division sentence to find the missing number.

__ x 4 = 12

12 ÷ __ = 4

12 ÷ 3 = 4, so _3_ x 4 = 12

7 x _6_ = 42

____ x 12 = 12

____ x 5 = 10

____ x 8 = 64

4 x ____ = 36

9 x ____ = 54

3 x ____ = 12

Racing Riddle

Divide to find the **quotient**.
Use your answers to decode the answer to the question.

$72 \div 9 =$ _____ **A**

$49 \div 7 =$ _____ **T**

$27 \div 3 =$ _____ **E**

$70 \div 7 =$ _____ **D**

$4 \div 4 =$ _____ **R**

$30 \div 6 =$ _____ **O**

$36 \div 9 =$ _____ **C**

$21 \div 7 =$ _____ **P**

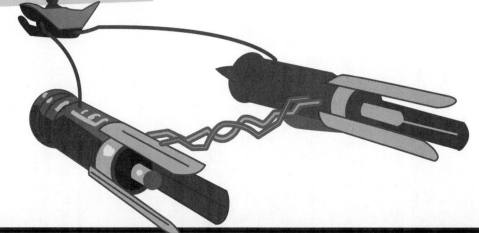

Question:

What did Anakin race to win
his freedom from slavery?

Answer:

__ __ __ __ __ __ __ __
3 5 10 1 8 4 9 1

Missing Data

Read each word problem. Write an equation using n for the number. Then solve.

C-3PO accidentally enters the droid assembly line on Geonosis. If he sees **48** droids in **8** equal rows, how many droids are in each row?

$48 \div 8 = n$ ___6___ droids

If C-3PO can learn **9** new languages every minute, how many languages can he learn in **10** minutes?

_____   _____ languages

If Jedi apprentice Anakin practices his skills for **4** hours each day, how many hours will he practice in **7** days?

_____   _____ hours

Droids are packing **72** comlinks in boxes. If they put **9** comlinks in each box, how many boxes will they have?

_____ _____ boxes

This mouse droid is fast! It can clean **5** floors of a starship in an hour. If it works for **20** hours, how many floors can it clean?

_____ _____ floors

Imagine that a squad is made up of **4** types of clones, and there are **9** sets of each type of clone. How many clones will the squad have?

_____ _____ clones

If Jabba the Hutt's palace has **80** rooms, and **2** people are sitting in each room, then how many people are sitting in his palace?

_____ _____ people

Two-Step Word Problems

Read each two-step word problem. Then solve.

On the cold planet of Hoth, people need goggles. Imagine that a goggle shop has **9** shelves and each shelf has **10** goggles on it. If **15** people buy goggles today, then how many goggles are left?

Step 1: **9** shelves with **10** goggles on a shelf

$9 \times 10 = \underline{90}$

Step 2: **15** goggles are sold

$90 - 15 = \underline{75}$

$\underline{75}$ goggles

The Empire is searching for the rebel base. Imagine that they have **100** probe droids, but **55** are on patrol. If the rest are sent out equally between **5** planets, how many does each planet get?

Step 1: _____

Step 2: _____

_____ droids

Imagine that a wampa captures **12** ice rats and **16** snow lizards. The wampa's **7** friends each eat the same number of animals until all the animals are gone. How many animals does each wampa get?

Step 1: _____

Step 2: _____

_____ animals

Imagine that R2-D2 works to repair his gadgets at the rebel base. He works on **6** gadgets each hour for **4** hours.
If he fixes **17** of them, how many gadgets were not fixed?

Step 1: _____

Step 2: _____

_____ gadgets

Imagine that R2-D2 has only **5** batteries left, so he collected **10** more packs of batteries. If there are **8** batteries in each pack, then how many batteries does R2-D2 have now?

Step 1: _____

Step 2: _____

_____ batteries

Imagine that Yoda is repairing his hut on Dagobah. He has **13** new stones. If today he finds and saves **5** new stones **5** times, how many stones will Yoda have in all?

Step 1: _____

Step 2: _____

_____ stones

Imagine that Luke is training. He uses the Force to move **4** rocks each into **8** stacks. Then he stacks **9** more rocks. How many rocks are stacked in all?

Step 1: _____

Step 2: _____

_____ rocks

Fraction Shapes

We can divide a whole into equal and unequal parts.

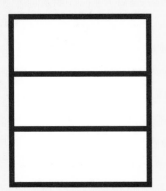
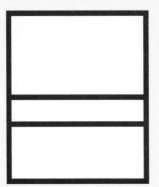

1 whole in
3 equal parts

1 whole in
3 unequal parts

A **unit fraction** is one of the equal parts of a whole.

1 equal part
3 equal parts of the whole

$$\frac{1}{3}$$

Are the shapes below divided into equal parts?

If so, color one of the equal parts and write the unit fraction.

If not, cross out the shape.

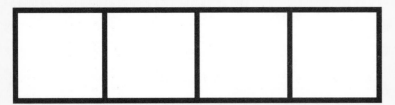

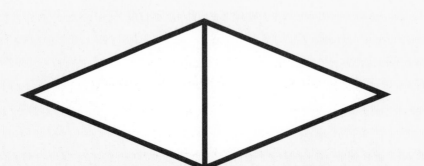

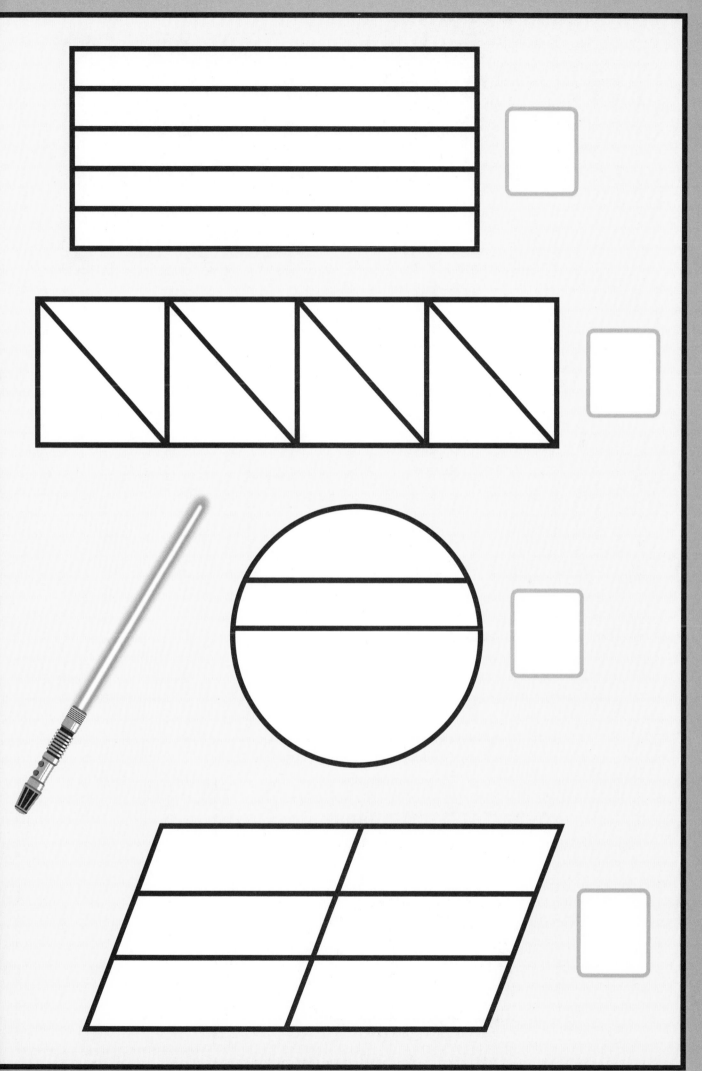

Scrap Work

A fraction has a **numerator** and a **denominator**.

$$\frac{1}{3}$$
← numerator
← denominator

Imagine that you are Watto working on scrap parts. Slice the figures into the number of parts named by the denominator. Then shade one part to show a unit fraction.

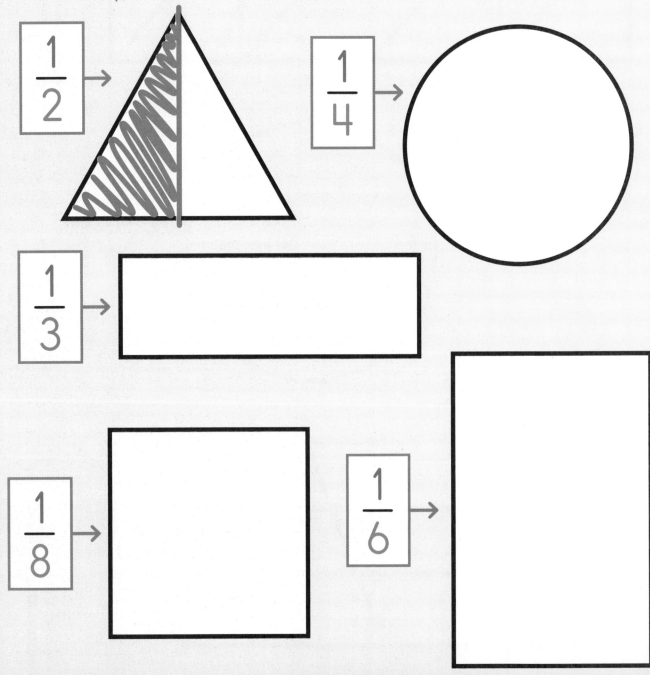

$\frac{1}{2}$ →

$\frac{1}{4}$ →

$\frac{1}{3}$ →

$\frac{1}{8}$ →

$\frac{1}{6}$ →

Slice the figures into the number of
parts named by the denominator.
Then shade the number of parts
named in the numerator.

$\dfrac{2}{3}$ →

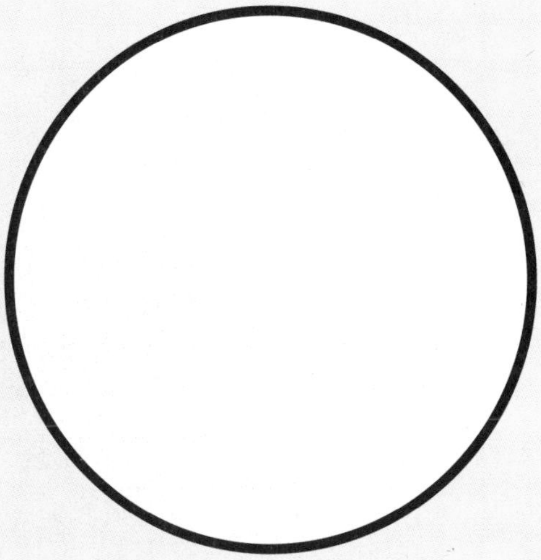

← $\dfrac{2}{4}$

$\dfrac{5}{6}$ →

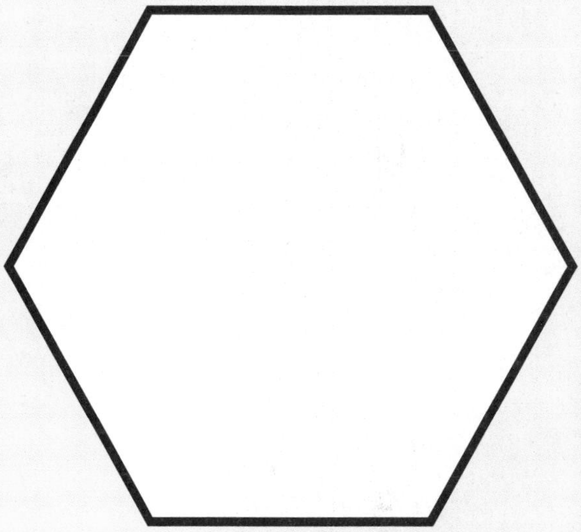

← $\dfrac{3}{8}$

$\dfrac{5}{8}$ →

Distance From Zero

You can show fractions on a **number line**.
The distance from 0 to 1 is divided into equal parts.

Imagine that Luke's training swamp on Dagobah is
1 kilometer long and divided into equal parts. How far
did Luke swing? Mark the point with a dot and write the faction.

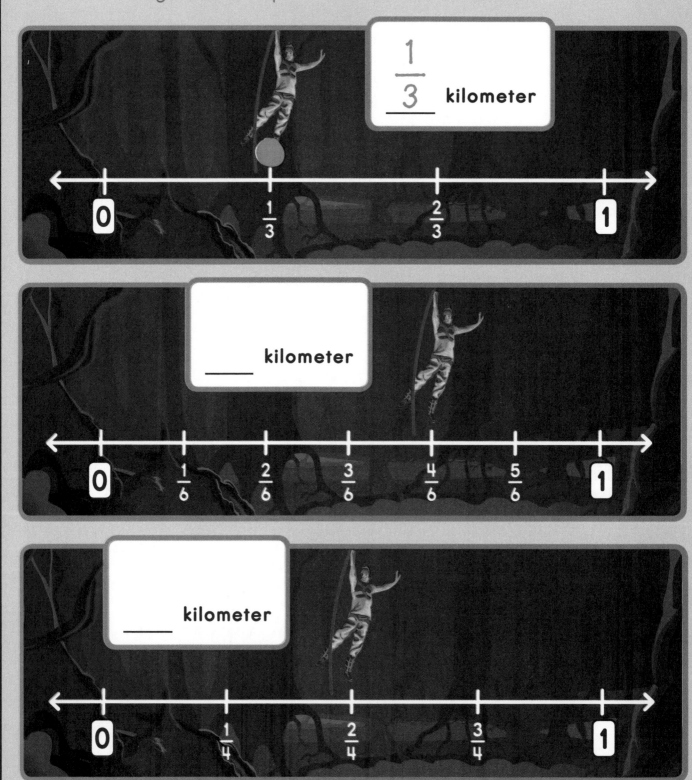

$\dfrac{1}{3}$ **kilometer**

0   $\dfrac{1}{3}$ $\dfrac{2}{3}$ 1

_____ **kilometer**

0   $\dfrac{1}{6}$ $\dfrac{2}{6}$ $\dfrac{3}{6}$ $\dfrac{4}{6}$ $\dfrac{5}{6}$ 1

_____ **kilometer**

0   $\dfrac{1}{4}$ $\dfrac{2}{4}$ $\dfrac{3}{4}$ 1

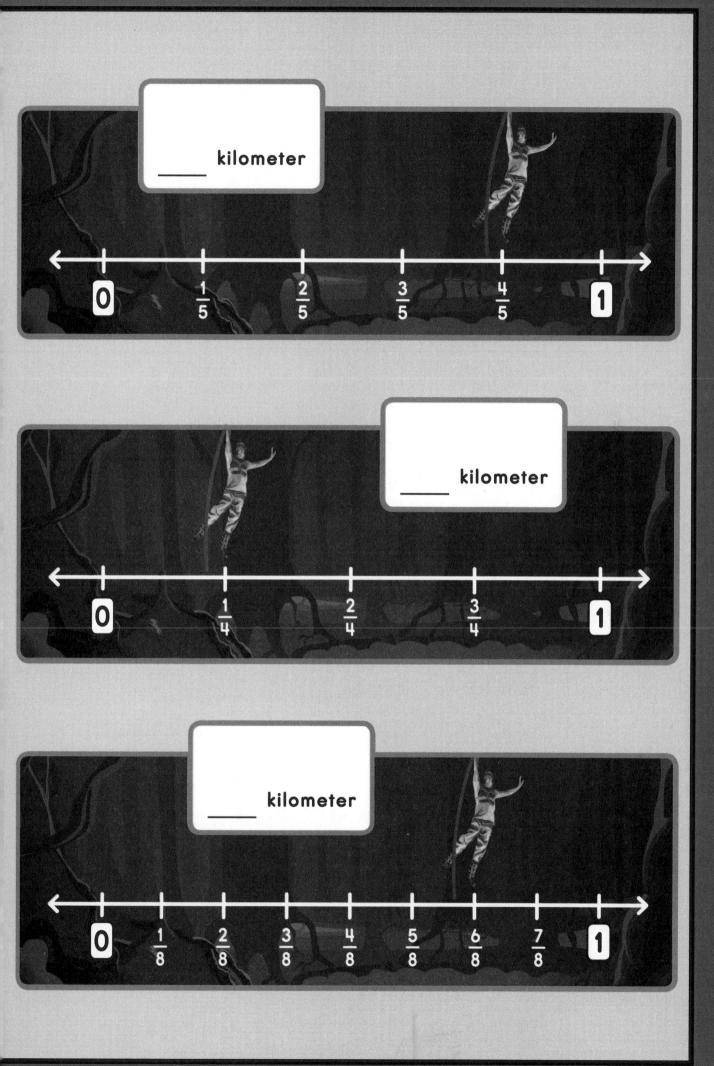

_____ kilometer

0   1/5   2/5   3/5   4/5   1

_____ kilometer

0   1/4   2/4   3/4   1

_____ kilometer

0   1/8   2/8   3/8   4/8   5/8   6/8   7/8   1

Fractions Power

Equivalent fractions name the same part of a whole.

Color the meters on the power droid so they are all $\frac{1}{2}$ filled.

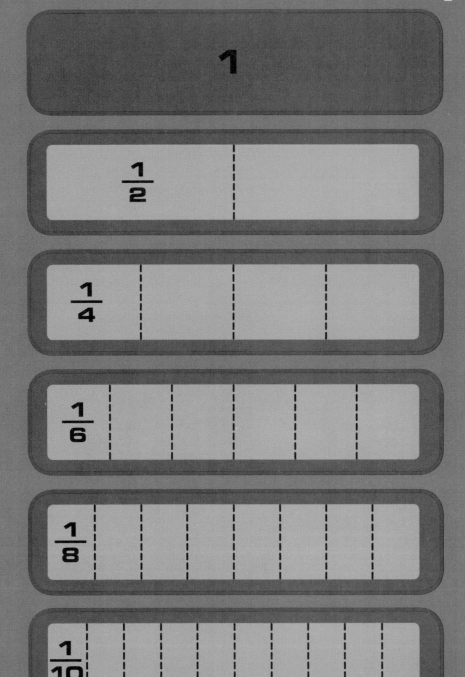

Fill in the missing numerators so each fraction is equivalent to $\frac{1}{2}$.

$$\frac{1}{2} = \frac{}{4} \qquad \frac{1}{2} = \frac{}{6} \qquad \frac{1}{2} = \frac{}{8} \qquad \frac{1}{2} = \frac{}{10}$$

Color the meters on the power droid so they are both $\frac{1}{3}$ filled.

$\frac{1}{3}$

$\frac{1}{6}$

Color the meters on the power droid so they are both $\frac{1}{4}$ filled.

$\frac{1}{4}$

$\frac{1}{8}$

Fill in the missing numerators so the fractions are equivalent.

$$\frac{1}{3} = \frac{}{6}$$ $$\frac{2}{3} = \frac{}{6}$$ $$\frac{1}{4} = \frac{}{8}$$

$$\frac{2}{4} = \frac{}{8}$$ $$\frac{3}{4} = \frac{}{8}$$

Fraction Names for One

On Jakku, Rey scavenged for scrap metal to earn food portions. The food was divided into equal slices. How many slices are in each piece of food? Count the parts. Write the fraction.

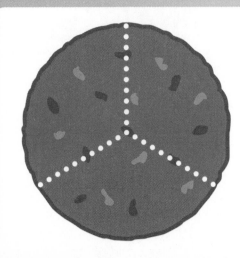

1 whole = ___3___ thirds

$$1 = \frac{3}{3}$$

___3___ slices

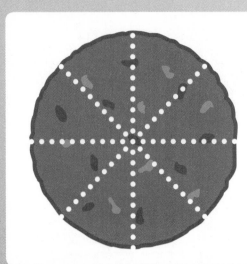

1 whole = _____ eighths

$$1 = \frac{}{}$$

_____ slices

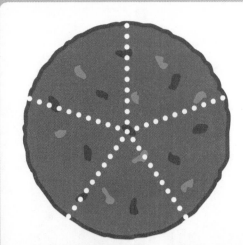

1 whole = _____ fifths

$$1 = \frac{}{}$$

_____ slices

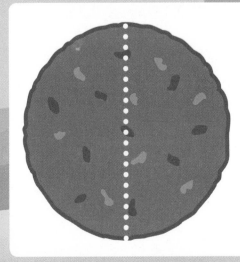

1 whole = _____ halves

$1 = \dfrac{}{}$

_____ slices

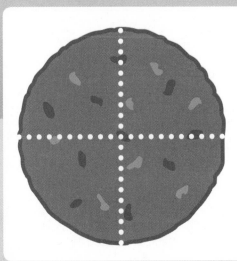

1 whole = _____ fourths

$1 = \dfrac{}{}$

_____ slices

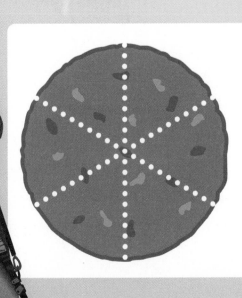

1 whole = _____ sixths

$1 = \dfrac{}{}$

_____ slices

Landing Zones

Shade the areas of each landing zone to find **equivalent fractions**.

Shade $\frac{2}{3}$ of each zone.

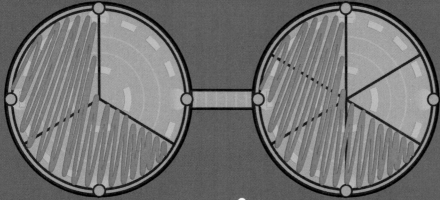

What fraction is equivalent to $\frac{2}{3}$? Complete the equation: $\frac{2}{3} = \frac{4}{6}$

Shade $\frac{3}{4}$ of each zone.

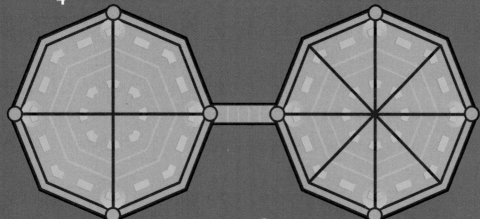

What fraction is equivalent to $\frac{3}{4}$? Complete the equation: $\frac{3}{4} = \frac{\quad}{\quad}$

Shade $\frac{2}{2}$ of Tiplar's landing zone. Shade $\frac{4}{4}$ of Tiplee's landing zone.

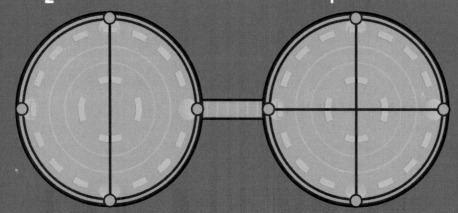

What fraction is equivalent to $\frac{2}{2}$? Complete the equation: $\frac{2}{2} = \frac{\quad}{\quad}$

Star Destroyer Math

The Star Destroyer flies through the galaxy. The planets it passes are represented by the whole numbers on the number line.

Color the whole number planets. Then write the fraction for each whole number greater than 0.

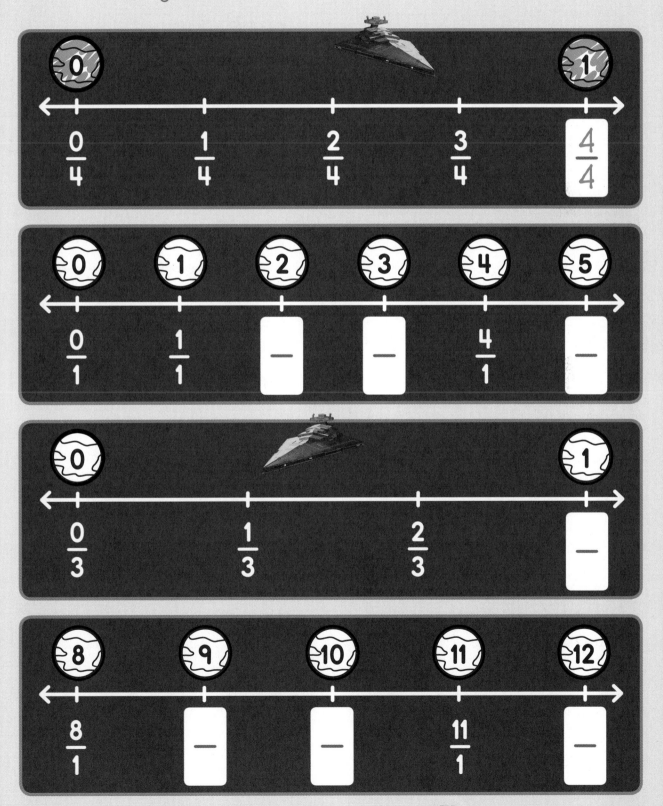

$\frac{0}{4}$ $\frac{1}{4}$ $\frac{2}{4}$ $\frac{3}{4}$ $\frac{4}{4}$

$\frac{0}{1}$ $\frac{1}{1}$ $-$ $-$ $\frac{4}{1}$ $-$

$\frac{0}{3}$ $\frac{1}{3}$ $\frac{2}{3}$ $-$

$\frac{8}{1}$ $-$ $-$ $\frac{11}{1}$ $-$

Comparing Fractions

The power cells below are only a fraction full. Compare the cells and write **greater** or **less** so each math sentence is true.

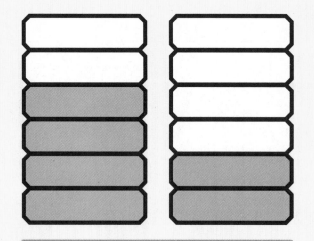

$$\frac{4}{6} \text{ is } \rule{2cm}{0.4pt} \text{ than } \frac{2}{6}$$

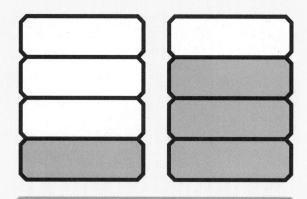

$$\frac{1}{4} \text{ is } \rule{2cm}{0.4pt} \text{ than } \frac{3}{4}$$

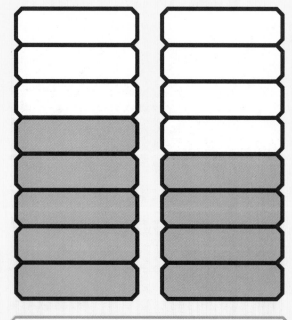

$$\frac{5}{8} \text{ is } \rule{2cm}{0.4pt} \text{ than } \frac{4}{8}$$

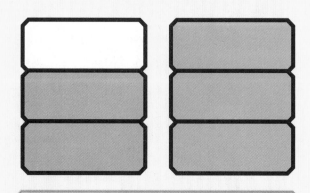

$$\frac{2}{3} \text{ is } \rule{2cm}{0.4pt} \text{ than } \frac{3}{3}$$

Color the cells to represent each fraction. Then compare the cells and write **greater** or **less** so each math sentence is true.

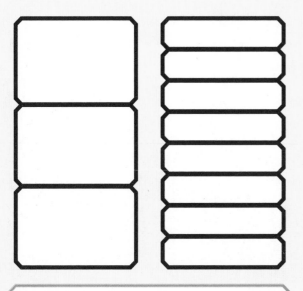

$\frac{2}{3}$ is _____ than $\frac{2}{8}$

$\frac{2}{6}$ is _____ than $\frac{2}{3}$

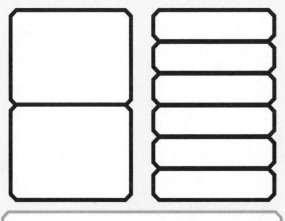

$\frac{1}{2}$ is _____ than $\frac{1}{6}$

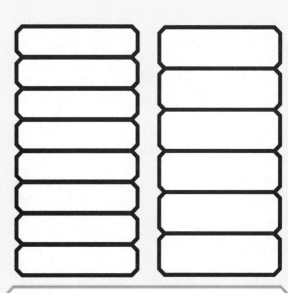

$\frac{2}{8}$ is _____ than $\frac{2}{6}$

Comparing Asteroid Clusters

> means greater than	= means equal to	< means less than
$\frac{1}{4} > \frac{1}{8}$	$\frac{1}{2} = \frac{2}{4}$	$\frac{1}{8} < \frac{1}{4}$

In each asteroid cluster, color the fractions that will make the statements true.

$\frac{3}{8}$ < blue fractions

$\frac{2}{8}$

$\frac{5}{8}$

$\frac{7}{7}$

$\frac{2}{4}$ > red fractions

$\frac{2}{3}$

$\frac{1}{4}$

$\frac{2}{2}$

$\frac{2}{8}$

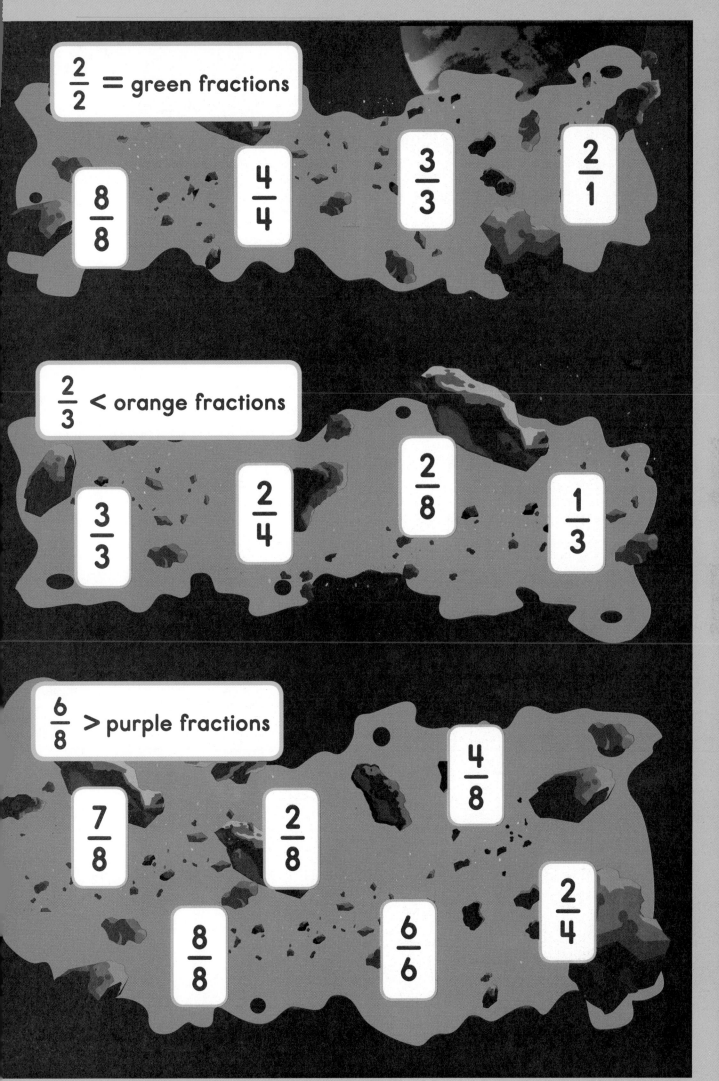

$\frac{2}{2}$ = green fractions

$\frac{8}{8}$

$\frac{4}{4}$

$\frac{3}{3}$

$\frac{2}{1}$

$\frac{2}{3}$ < orange fractions

$\frac{3}{3}$

$\frac{2}{4}$

$\frac{2}{8}$

$\frac{1}{3}$

$\frac{6}{8}$ > purple fractions

$\frac{7}{8}$

$\frac{2}{8}$

$\frac{4}{8}$

$\frac{8}{8}$

$\frac{6}{6}$

$\frac{2}{4}$

Telling Time

Skip count by fives to tell time. Fill in the time. Write a.m. or p.m.

The hour hand is between 7 and 8.
Count 5, 10, 15, 20, 25 for the minute hand.

Wake up:

<u>7</u> : <u>10</u> <u>a.m.</u>

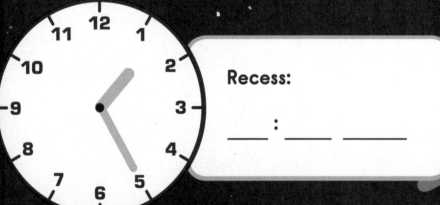

Recess:

___ : ___ ___

After-school music lessons:

___ : ___ ___

Reading before bedtime:

___ : ___ ___

Time Matching

Count by fives and ones to tell time to the minute.

The hour hand is between 1 and 2. For the minute hand, count 5, 10, 15; then continue counting: 16, 17.

1:17 p.m.

Draw a line from the clock to the time it shows.

5:33

5:06

5:11

5:46

5:21

Time Travels

Imagine that you are on a journey through the galaxy in the *Millennium Falcon*. Draw hands on the clocks to show the time you would arrive on each planet.

It is **7:46** when you arrive on Jakku.

It is **3:17** when you arrive on Hoth.

It is **11:12** when you arrive on Tatooine.

It is **6:57** when you arrive on Naboo.

It is **12:33** when you arrive on Dagobah.

What time is it on your planet? Fill in the blanks and draw hands on the clock. Then draw a picture of your planet.

It is ____:____ on _____.

Time Tales

Imagine that it's your job to watch the clock to solve each word problem. Write the **elapsed time** on the line.

Young Anakin began to clean Watto's shop at 4:54 p.m. He finished at 5:10 p.m. How long did he work?

16 minutes

A sandstorm on Tatooine began at 9:04 a.m. and lasted for 1 hour and 6 minutes. What time was it when the storm ended?

_____

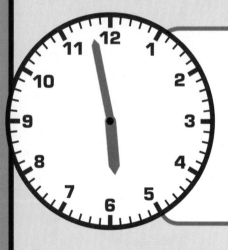

Anakin spent 1 hour and 22 minutes fixing C-3PO. He finished his repairs at 5:58 p.m. At what time did he begin the repairs?

_____

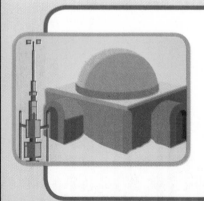

Anakin's mom begins fixing a hose at the moisture farm at 6:12 p.m. If it takes her 33 minutes to finish, when is she done?

_____

Qui-Gon Jinn has a half-hour conversation with young Anakin. They sat down to talk at 11:19 a.m. At what time did their conversation end?

_____

Anakin worked on his podracer from 6:23 a.m. until 8:34 a.m. How long did he work on his podracer?

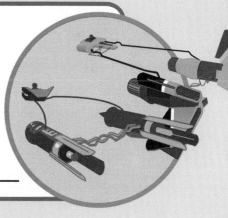

_____

The podrace will begin in 19 minutes. It is 10:26 a.m. now. At what time will the race begin?

_____

Anakin slept for 8 hours and 5 minutes. If he woke up at 5:36 a.m., at what time did he fall asleep?

_____

Cantina Containers

This water bottle holds about **1 liter (L)** of liquid.

Estimate how much each of the other containers hold.

Color the container red if it holds less than 1 liter.
Color the container purple if it holds more than 1 liter.
Color the container blue if it holds about 1 liter.

Use the pictures to help you solve the problems. **L** stands for **liter**. Write the equation. Then solve.

Imagine Luke Skywalker had **5** liters of blue milk. After he drank some blue milk, he has this much left. How many liters of blue milk did Luke drink?

[ ] **liters**

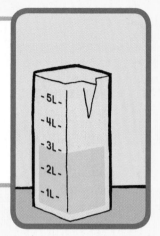

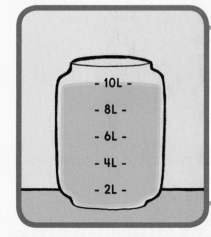

Imagine that Mos Eisley made the Darth Malted Milkshake in this picture. How much did Mos make in all?

[ ] **liters**

Imagine Chewbacca ordered the **4** chocolate milk drinks in this picture. How many liters of chocolate milk did Chewbacca order?

[ ] **liters**

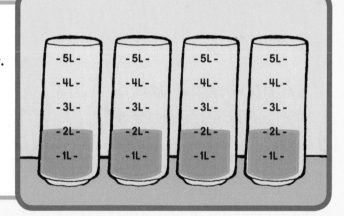

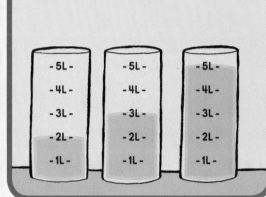

Imagine this container of Green Apple Yoda Soda was shared equally by **5** aliens. How many liters did each alien get?

[ ] **liters**

Mass Matters

The basic metric units of mass are the **gram** and **kilogram**.

About **1 gram (g)**

1 battle droid
antenna

**1,000 grams =
1 kilogram (kg)**

1,000 battle droid
antennas

1 kilogram (kg)

1 battle droid
head

A mouse droid is used for cleaning and carrying messages.
The mouse droid measures objects that are easy to lift in **grams**.
It measures objects that are hard to lift in **kilograms**.

Write gram or kilogram to help this mouse droid
know which unit to use.

A small circuit board
should be measured in

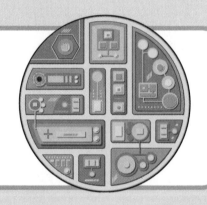

__grams__ .

A broken probe droid
should be measured in

_____ .

A bearing from a podracer should be measured in

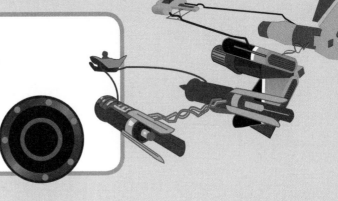

_____.

A pair of binoculars from Tatooine should be measured in

_____.

Stormtrooper armor should be measured in

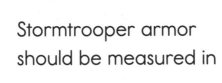

_____.

A lightsaber should be measured in

_____.

Poe's life support box should be measured in

_____.

Padawan Participants

The picture graph shows how many Padawans of each species are in the Jedi Training Academy. The key shows how to read the symbols in the picture graph.

Padawans in the Jedi Training Academy

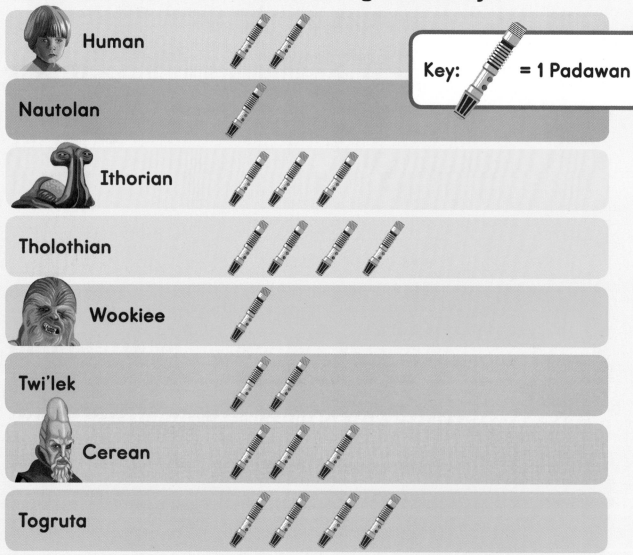

Key: = 1 Padawan

The following younglings join the school. Draw lightsabers to complete the picture graph.

| Wookiee: 1 | Twi'lek: 2 | Cerean: 3 | Togruta: 4 |

Which species has the most Padawans?

How many Padawans do they have?

Which species has the fewest Padawans?

How many Padawans do they have?

How many more Padawans are Cerean than Wookiee?

How many Padawans in all are Ithorian or Twi'lek?

How many more Padawans are Togruta than Tholothian?

You would also like to join the Jedi Training Academy. Draw one more lightsaber in the correct row to complete the picture graph.

Bar Graphs

This **bar graph** shows the number of major cities on each planet.
The **vertical scale** (that runs bottom to top) is in units of 2.

Look at the top of each bar to see how many major cities are on each planet.

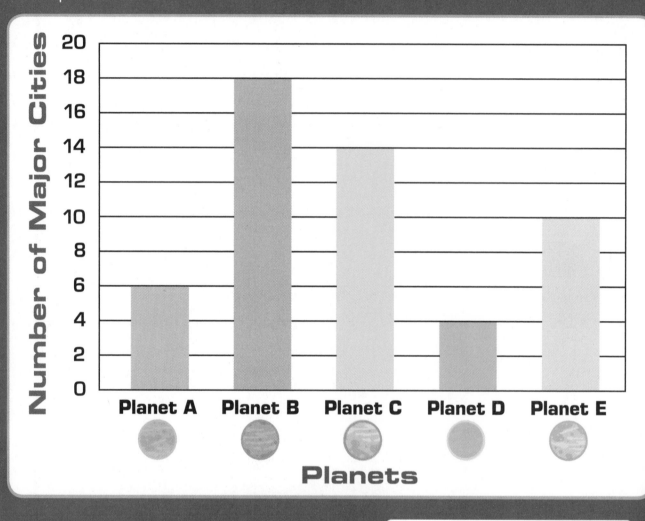

How many major cities are on Planet C?

14 cities

How many major cities are on Planet E?

How many more major cities are on
Planet B than on Planet A?

How many major cities are on the 2 planets
that have the fewest number of major cities?

This bar graph shows the same data with a **horizontal scale** (that runs left to right). The horizontal scale is in units of 2.

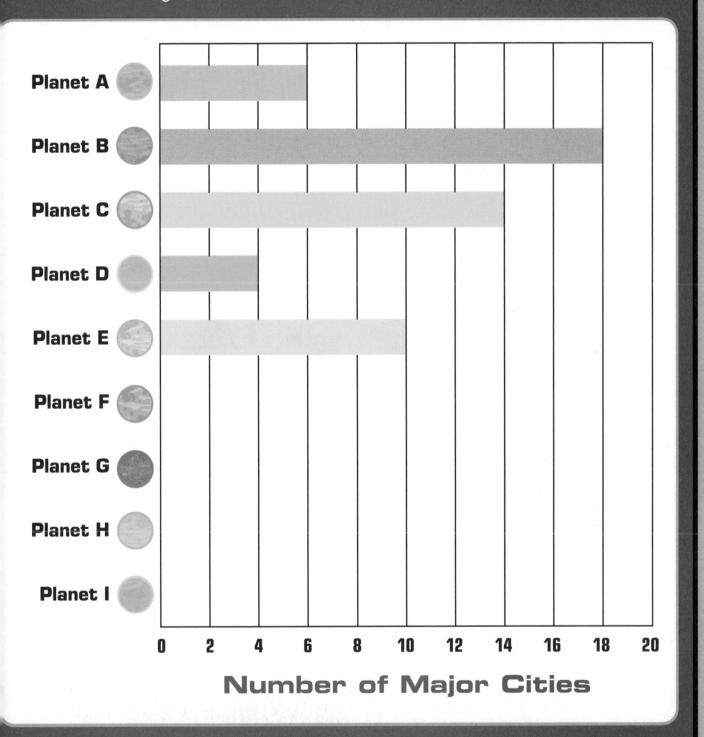

Number of Major Cities

Four more planets were added to the list.
Draw and color bars to complete the graph.

Planet F: 16 major cities
Planet G: 14 major cities
Planet H: 6 major cities
Planet I: 10 major cities

Hero Hobbies

Imagine you collected data on the heroes' hobbies from the *Star Wars* saga. Answer the questions or fill in the blanks using the data in the bar graphs.

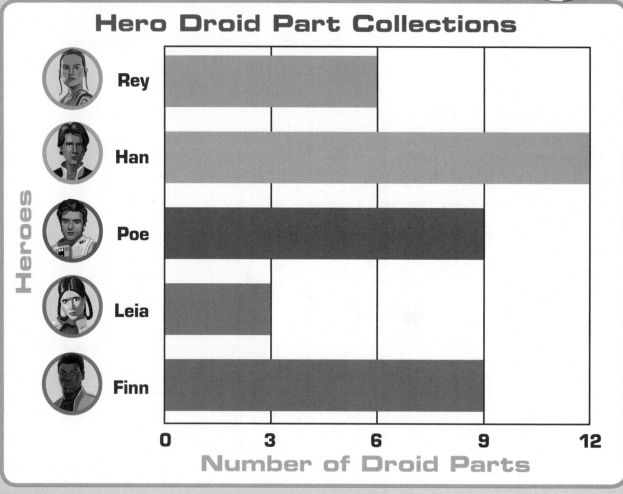

How many parts did Rey and Finn collect together?

_____ **parts**

How many more parts would Leia have to collect to catch up with Rey?

_____ **parts**

If you collected 4 times as many droid parts as Poe, how many droid parts would you collect?

_____ **parts**

Who collected more droid parts, Han and Leia or Poe and Finn?

_____ **and** _____

How much more did they collect than the other pair?

_____ **more parts**

Favorite Topics to Read

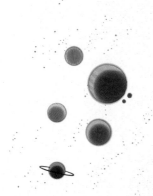

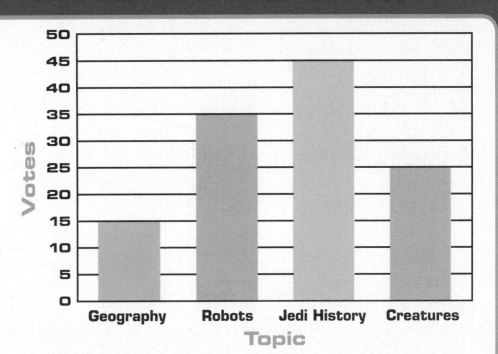

60 rebels said that geography and _____ are their favorite topics to read.

60 other rebels also said that _____ and _____ are their favorite topics to read.

Points Scored by Ezra in a Flight Simulator

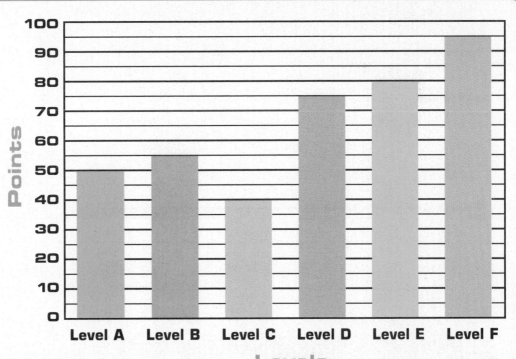

What is the difference between Ezra's highest and lowest score? _____ **points**

If Ezra scores 3 times as high on Level G as he did on Level E, what will his score be? _____ **points**

Measure the Starship Parts

Astromech droids fix the tiniest parts on starships. Now it's your turn. Measure the length of these starship parts to the nearest half inch.

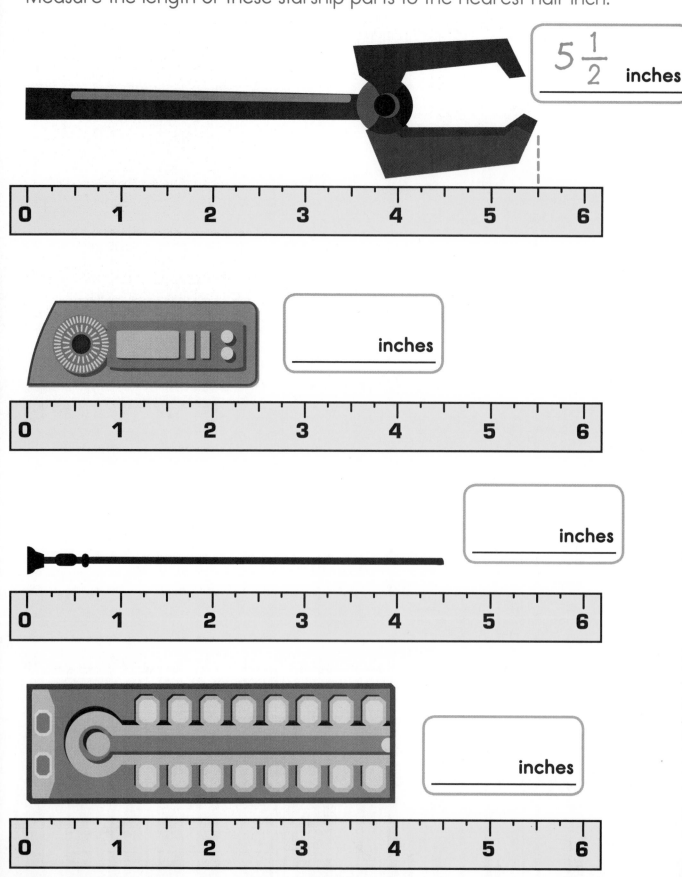

$5\frac{1}{2}$ _____ inches

_____ inches

_____ inches

_____ inches

Write your measurements from page 68 at the end of the astromech droid's list.

1, 3, 3, $2\frac{1}{2}$, $2\frac{1}{2}$, $4\frac{1}{2}$, 3, 3, 6, 1, _____ , _____ , _____ , _____

How many starship parts are there of each length?

1 inch: _____ $2\frac{1}{2}$ inches: _____   3 inches: _____   4 inches: _____

$4\frac{1}{2}$ inches: _____ $5\frac{1}{2}$ inches: _____   6 inches: _____

The **line plot** below is labeled from 1 to 6 in half-inch units because the shortest starship part is 1 inch and the longest is 6 inches. Each **X** stands for one starship part. The number of **X**s is the total number of starship parts that have that measurement.

Write an **X** for the total number of starship parts of each length.

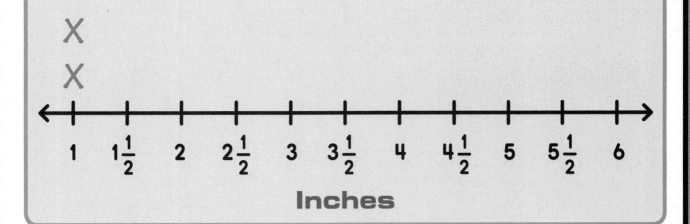

Starship Parts of Each Length

Inches

Area Argument

To find the **area** of a region, count the number of **unit squares** that cover it without overlapping or leaving gaps. A unit square or **square unit** is a square with side lengths that are 1 unit each. The unit can be any measurement of length, like inches, feet, or meters.

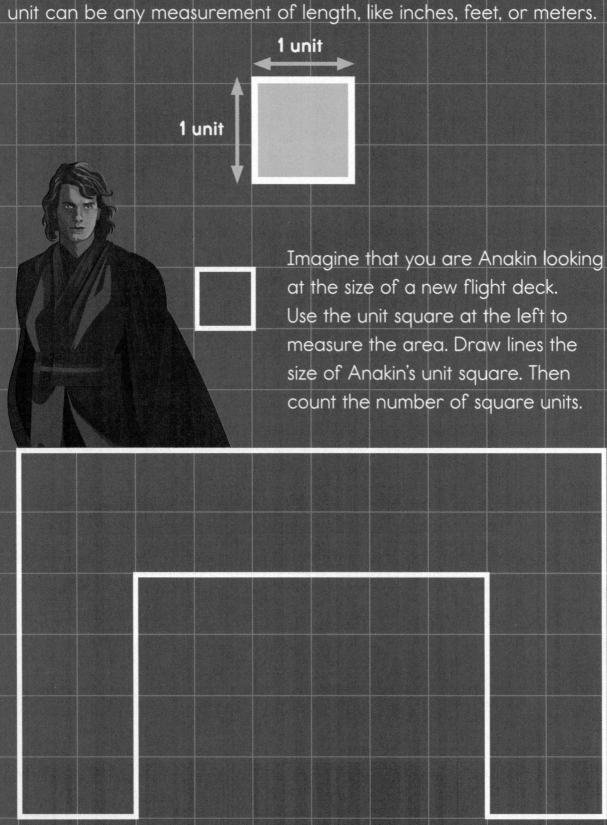

1 unit

1 unit

Imagine that you are Anakin looking at the size of a new flight deck. Use the unit square at the left to measure the area. Draw lines the size of Anakin's unit square. Then count the number of square units.

Imagine that you are C-3PO looking at the same new flight deck. Use the unit square to the right to measure the area. Draw lines the size of C-3PO's unit square. Then count the number of square units.

C-3PO and Anakin disagree about the number of square units in the floor of his flight deck.

Write each of their numbers of unit squares.

Anakin's way: [ ]   C-3PO's way: [ ]

Both answers are correct. The area depends on the size of the unit.

Sandboxes

The Tusken Raiders are planning to set up new camps.

This yellow camp covers 9 unit squares, so it has an area of 9 square units.

The green camp also has an area of 9 square units.

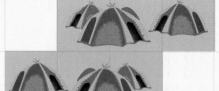

> Color in 5 camp areas that are each 12 square units but have different shapes.

Color in 6 camp areas that are each 16 square units but have different shapes.

Find the Area

Count the unit squares to find the area of each object.

Include the unit measurement in your answer.

Imagine that each square of R2-D2's holoscreen is 1 square meter.

Area =

_____

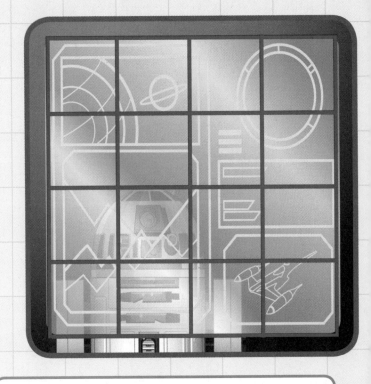

Imagine that each square of Darth Vader's chest box is 1 square centimeter.

Area =

_____

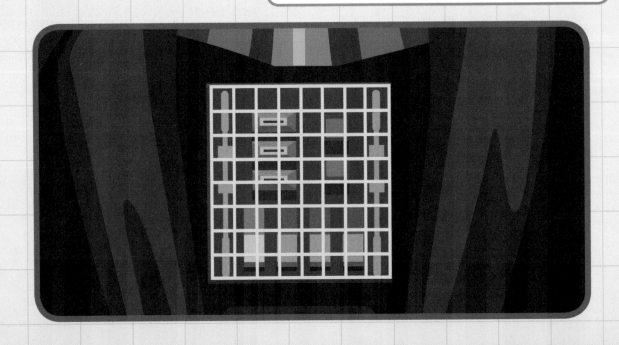

Imagine that each square of the lightsaber is 1 square centimeter.

Area = _____

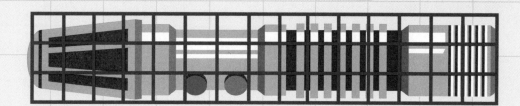

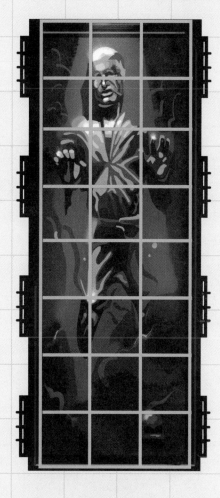

Imagine that each square of Han Solo's carbonite is 1 square foot.

Area = _____

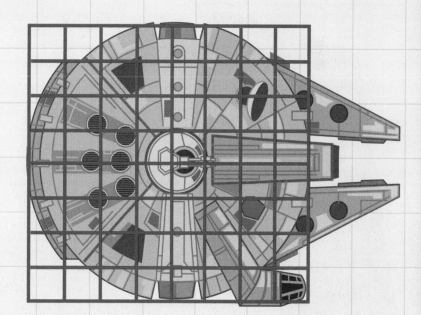

Imagine that each square of *Millennium Falcon*'s main hull is 1 square meter.

Area = _____

Area by Multiplication

You can find the area of a rectangle by counting the unit squares.

| 1 | 2 | 3 | 4 |
| 5 | 6 | 7 | 8 |

8 square units

OR

You can find the area of a rectangle by multiplying its length by its width.

2 x 4 = **8 square units**

4 units

2 units

| 1 | 2 | 3 | 4 |
| 5 | 6 | 7 | 8 |

Imagine Rey is boxing this scrap metal. Find the area of each box by multiplying length times width. Include the square unit measurement in your answer.

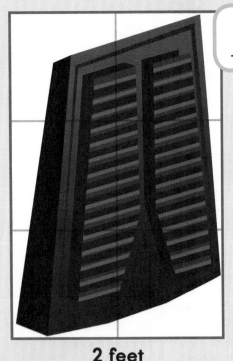

3 feet

2 feet

3 x 2 = 6 square feet

10 inches

10 inches

___ x ___ = _____

13 inches

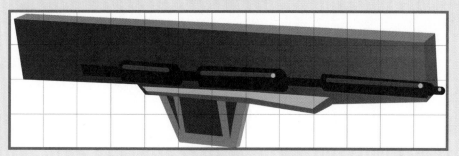

4 inches

_____ x _____ = _____

_____ x _____ = _____

4 inches

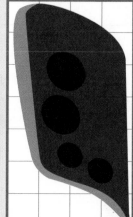

7 inches

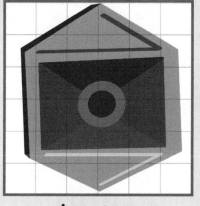

6 meters

6 meters

_____ x _____ = _____

3 feet

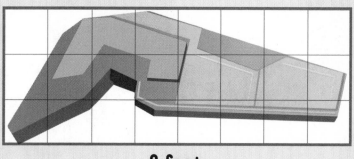

8 feet

_____ x _____ = _____

Area Matching

The space station has been attacked and debris is everywhere! Calculate the area of each panel and match it to the correct area number.

7 meters

7 meters

48 square meters

6 meters

8 meters

45 square meters

9 meters

6 meters

49 square meters

5 meters

9 meters

54 square meters

Help repair the space station by matching
panels that have the same area.

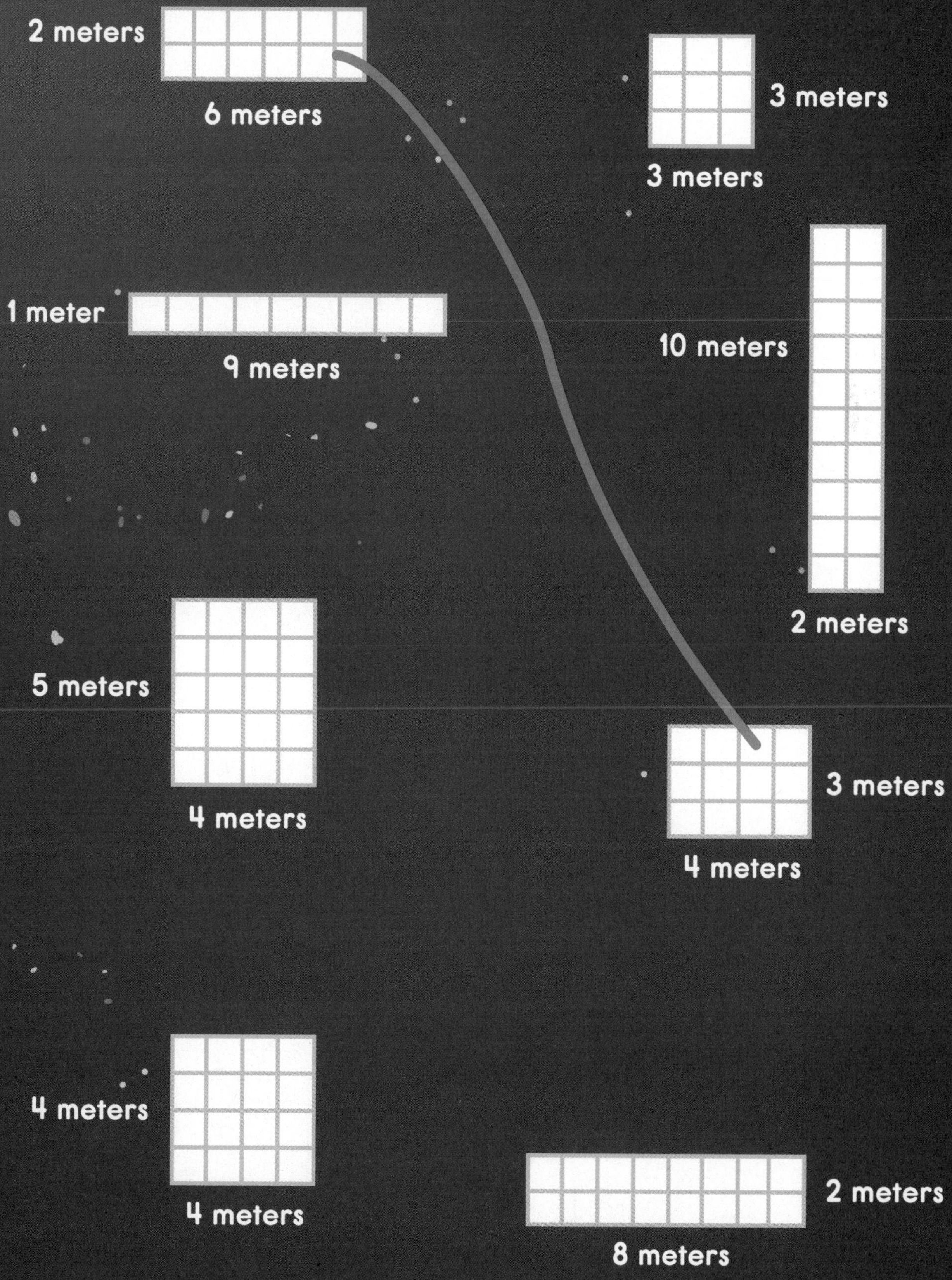

2 meters

6 meters

3 meters

3 meters

1 meter

9 meters

10 meters

2 meters

5 meters

4 meters

3 meters

4 meters

4 meters

4 meters

2 meters

8 meters

Get in Shape

Finn and Rey are planning an attack on the Starkiller Base compound.

Use the blueprints below to help them find the area of each room. Divide each room into two rectangles. Find the area of each new rectangle and add to get the total area.

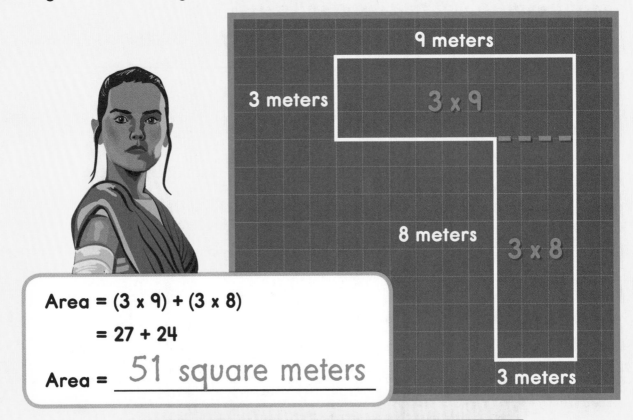

9 meters

3 meters

3 x 9

8 meters

3 x 8

3 meters

Area = (3 x 9) + (3 x 8)

= 27 + 24

Area = <u>51 square meters</u>

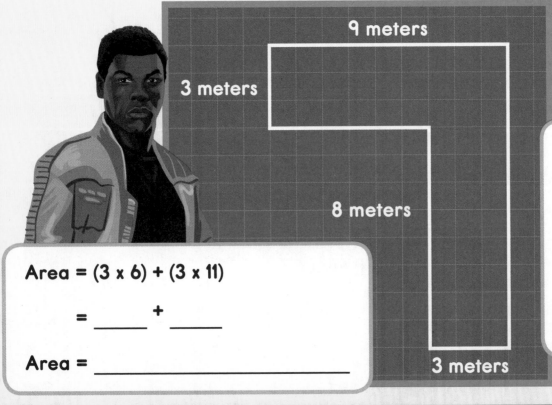

9 meters

3 meters

8 meters

3 meters

Is the area the same whichever way you divide the shape?

_____

Area = (3 x 6) + (3 x 11)

= ____ + ____

Area = _____

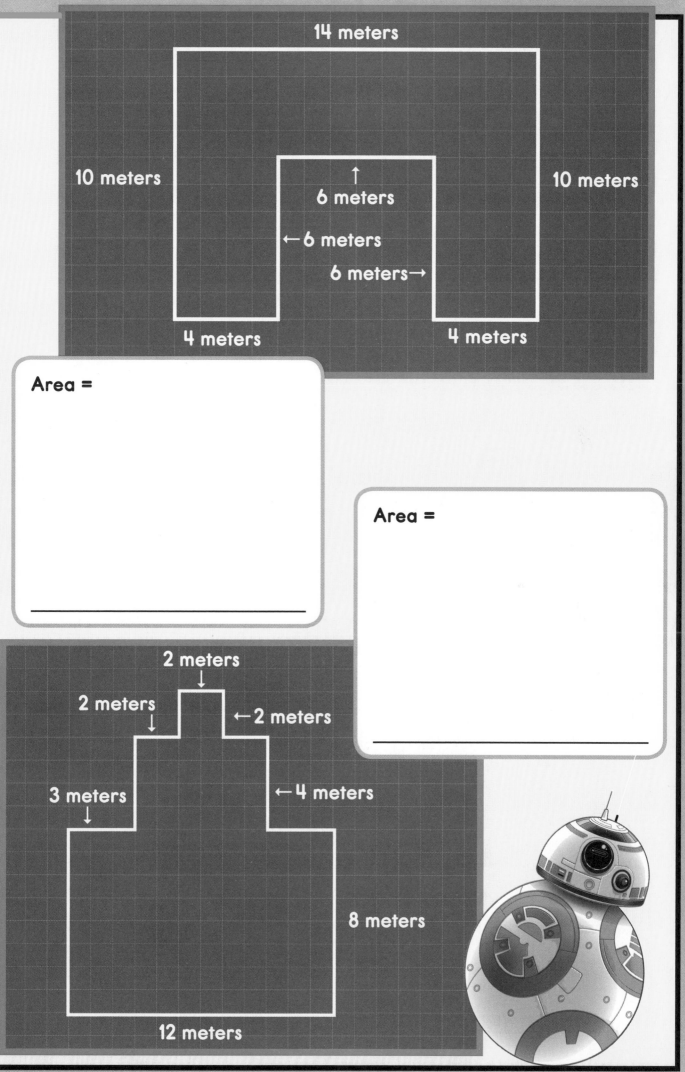

14 meters

10 meters   10 meters

↑
6 meters

←6 meters

6 meters→

4 meters   4 meters

Area =

Area =

2 meters
↓

2 meters   ←2 meters
↓

3 meters   ←4 meters
↓

8 meters

12 meters

Model Perimeters

The **perimeter** is the distance around the outside of a shape.

Add the side lengths to find the perimeter.

This rectangle has a perimeter of:

10 + 5 + 10 + 5 = 30 meters

10 meters

5 meters

5 meters

10 meters

Find the perimeter of these model plane parts.

8 inches

A TIE fighter wing has six equal sides. Each side is 8 inches.

Perimeter = <u>48 inches</u>

2 inches

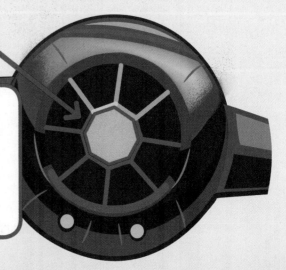

The center of a cockpit window has eight equal sides. Each side is 2 inches.

Perimeter = _____

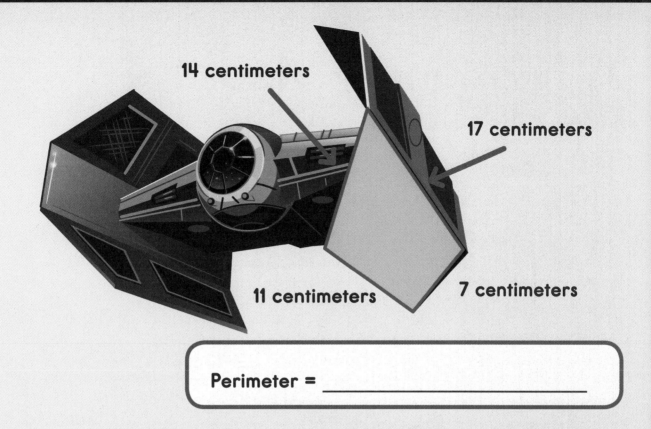

14 centimeters

17 centimeters

11 centimeters

7 centimeters

Perimeter = _____

Perimeter A = _____

2 centimeters

8 centimeters **A** 10 centimeters

5 centimeters

15 centimeters

8 centimeters **B**

17 centimeters

Perimeter B = _____

A Mission to Measure

Find the missing lengths of each shape.

3 feet

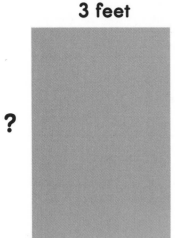

? ?

3 feet

Imagine that you are fixing the front cockpit glass of this X-wing. The perimeter of the glass is 20 feet. The width is 3 feet. The two missing sides are equal. Find the length of each of the missing sides.

_____ feet

Next, imagine that you are fixing the side cockpit glass of this X-wing. Its perimeter is 139 inches. Find the missing length.

_____ inches

31 inches   **45 inches**

?

5 inches

? ?

5 inches

Imagine that you are investigating the abdominal plate of Han's stormtrooper armor. It's a rectangle. The width is 5 inches. The perimeter is 16 inches. Find the length of the missing sides.

_____ inches

Next, imagine that you are fixing this air intake from a starship. The two longest sides of the hexagon are each 5 inches. The perimeter is 26 inches. The four missing sides are equal. Find the length of the missing sides.

_____inches

5 inches

5 inches

? ?

? ?

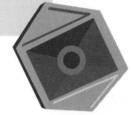

?

? ?

?

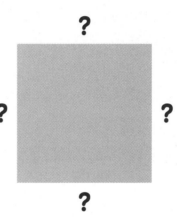

Imagine that this square circuit board also needs repair. The perimeter is 100 inches. How long is each side of the square circuit board?

_____ inches

Last, imagine that you are investigating this door on the Death Star. It has eight equal sides and a perimeter of 72 meters. How long is each side of the door?

_____ meters

?

? ?

? ?

? ?

?

The Jedi Way

Solve the area and perimeter problems. Use your answers to decode the answer to the question.

Imagine that healing herbs grow in plots that are 8 meters wide and 10 meters long. What is the area of each plot?

_____ square meters **P**

Imagine that a WANTED poster has a width of 20 centimeters and a length of 7 centimeters. What is the perimeter of this Galactic Empire poster?

_____ centimeters **D**

If an airshaft door is 9 feet on each side, what is the area of the door?

_____ square inches **A**

If a room in Maz Kanata's castle cellar is 6 meters wide and 7 meters long, what is the perimeter of the rooms?

_____ meters **N**

Imagine that a rebel starfighter's badge has a width of 9 centimeters and a length of 11 centimeters. What is the perimeter of the badge?

_____ centimeters **W**

What is the area of a climbing wall at the Imperial Academy, if it has a width of 10 meters and a length of 18 meters?

_____ square meters **E**

If a projection of a map piece is 8 centimeters wide and 6 centimeters tall, what is the area?

_____ square centimeters **L**

If a square window in Poe's X-wing fighter has a perimeter of 200 centimeters, how long is one side of the window?

_____ centimeters **R**

Question:

What do you call a youngling learning
the Jedi way?

Answer:

80	81	54	81	40	81	26
48	180	81	50	26	180	50

Shape Protocol

All quadrilaterals have 4 sides.

C-3PO is explaining the different types of **quadrilateral** shapes that make up a droid.

Read the definition of each shape.

Then draw your own version of that shape.

trapezoid

- Has 1 pair of parallel sides
- Sides are equal or unequal in length
- May have square corners

parallelogram

- Has 2 pairs of parallel sides
- Opposite sides are equal in length

rectangle

- A parallelogram with square corners

square

- A rectangle (and thus a parallelogram as well) with sides that are equal in length
- Has square corners

rhombus

- A parallelogram with all sides having equivalent measures
- No square corners

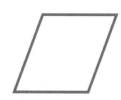 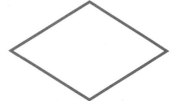

Draw a quadrilateral that fits the description. Then write its name.

Draw a quadrilateral that has two opposite sides of the same length, as well as two parallel sides.

Draw a quadrilateral that is a parallelogram and a rectangle.

Draw a quadrilateral with only 1 pair of parallel sides.

Draw a quadrilateral that has 2 pairs of parallel sides but is not a square.

Use the quadrilaterals above to draw your own droid.

Word Problems

Read each word problem. Then solve.

Imagine that Maz makes 32 liters of fruit punch. She divides the punch into 8 glasses. How many liters are in each glass?

_____ **liters**

Imagine there are 1358 stormtroopers ready for battle. If 600 more troopers join them, what is the total number of stormtroopers?

_____ **stormtroopers**

Imagine that Beru has 27 kilograms of rye and 41 kilograms of barley in storage bins. How much more barley than rye does she have?

_____ **kilograms**

Imagine that Han Solo finds 72 grams of spare wire. He uses 63 grams to fix his circuit board. How much does he have left?

_____ **grams**

Imagine that Chewbacca needs 10 spark plugs to repair the *Millennium Falcon*. Each spark plug has a mass of 9 grams. What is the total mass of the spark plugs?

_____ **grams**

Answers

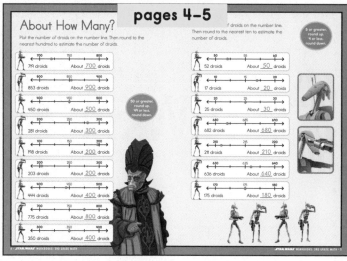

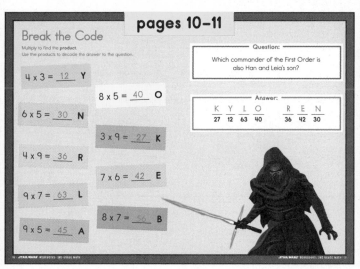

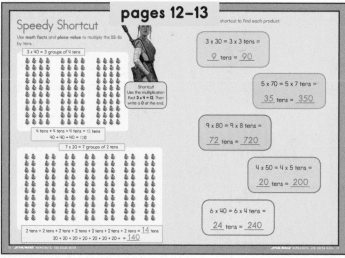

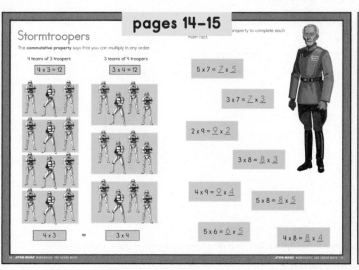

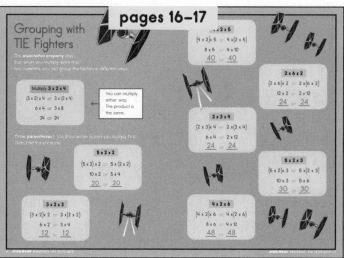

Answers

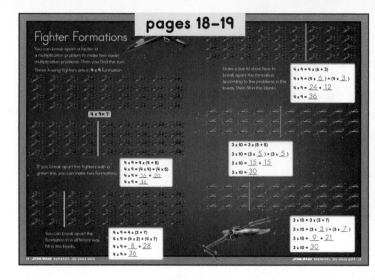

Fighter Formations

You can break apart a factor in a multiplication problem to make two easier multiplication problems. Then you find the sum.

These X-wing fighters are in 4 x 9 formation.

4 x 9 = ?

Draw a line to show how to break apart the formation according to the problems in the boxes. Then fill in the blanks.

$4 \times 9 = 4 \times (6 + 3)$
$4 \times 9 = (4 \times 6) + (4 \times 3)$
$4 \times 9 = 24 + 12$
$4 \times 9 = 36$

If you break apart the fighters with a green line, you can make two formations.
$4 \times 9 = 4 \times (4 + 5)$
$4 \times 9 = (4 \times 4) + (4 \times 5)$
$4 \times 9 = 16 + 20$
$4 \times 9 = 36$

$3 \times 10 = 3 \times (5 + 5)$
$3 \times 10 = (3 \times 5) + (3 \times 5)$
$3 \times 10 = 15 + 15$
$3 \times 10 = 30$

You can break apart the formation in a different way. Fill in the blanks.
$4 \times 9 = 4 \times (2 + 7)$
$4 \times 9 = (4 \times 2) + (4 \times 7)$
$4 \times 9 = 8 + 28$
$4 \times 9 = 36$

$3 \times 10 = 3 \times (3 + 7)$
$3 \times 10 = (3 \times 3) + (3 \times 7)$
$3 \times 10 = 9 + 21$
$3 \times 10 = 30$

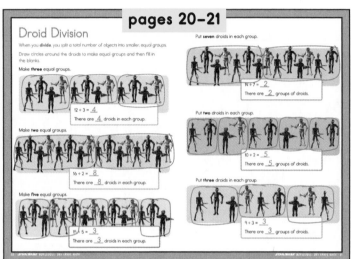

Droid Division

When you **divide**, you split a total number of objects into smaller, equal groups.

Draw circles around the droids to make equal groups and then fill in the blanks.

Make three equal groups.
$12 \div 3 = 4$
There are 4 droids in each group.

Make two equal groups.
$16 \div 2 = 8$
There are 8 droids in each group.

Make five equal groups.
$15 \div 5 = 3$
There are 3 droids in each group.

Put **seven** droids in each group.
$14 \div 7 = 2$
There are 2 groups of droids.

Put **two** droids in each group.
$10 \div 2 = 5$
There are 5 groups of droids.

Put **three** droids in each group.
$9 \div 3 = 3$
There are 3 groups of droids.

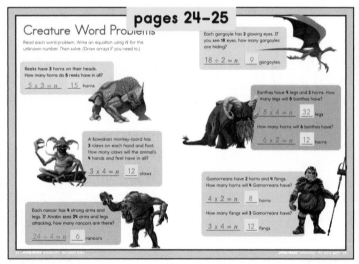

Forceful Formations

An **array** shows how multiplication and division are related fact families.

This array of clone troopers shows 3 groups of 5.
$3 \times 5 = 15$
The same array also shows 15 clone troopers divided into equal groups (rows) of 5. There are 3 rows.
$15 \div 5 = 3$

This array of clone troopers shows 5 groups of 3.
$5 \times 3 = 15$
The same array also shows 15 clone troopers divided into equal groups (columns) of 3. There are 5 columns.
$15 \div 3 = 5$

Identify the related facts that the array shows. Circle the groups. Then complete the equations.

$3 \times 6 = 18$
$18 \div 6 = 3$

$6 \times 3 = 18$
$18 \div 3 = 6$

$4 \times 7 = 28$
$28 \div 7 = 4$

$7 \times 4 = 28$
$28 \div 4 = 7$

$2 \times 8 = 16$
$16 \div 8 = 2$

$8 \times 2 = 16$
$16 \div 2 = 8$

Draw an array to show 2 groups of 9 clone troopers and 9 groups of 2 clone troopers. Write the related fact families.

$2 \times 9 = 18$
$18 \div 9 = 2$

$9 \times 2 = 18$
$18 \div 2 = 9$

Creature Word Problems

Read each word problem. Write an equation using n for the unknown number. Then solve. (Draw arrays if you need to.)

Reeks have 3 horns on their heads. How many horns do 5 reeks have in all?
$5 \times 3 = n$ 15 horns

A Kowakian monkey-lizard has 3 claws on each hand and foot. How many claws will the animal's 4 hands and feet have in all?
$3 \times 4 = n$ 12 claws

Each rancor has 4 strong arms and legs. If Anakin sees 24 arms and legs attacking, how many rancors are there?
$24 \div 4 = n$ 6 rancors

Each gargoyle has 2 glowing eyes. If you see 18 eyes, how many gargoyles are hiding?
$18 \div 2 = n$ 9 gargoyles

Banthas have 4 legs and 2 horns. How many legs will 8 banthas have?
$8 \times 4 = n$ 32 legs

How many horns will 6 banthas have?
$6 \times 2 = n$ 12 horns

Gamorreans have 2 horns and 4 fangs. How many horns will 4 Gamorreans have?
$4 \times 2 = n$ 8 horns

How many fangs will 3 Gamorreans have?
$3 \times 4 = n$ 12 fangs

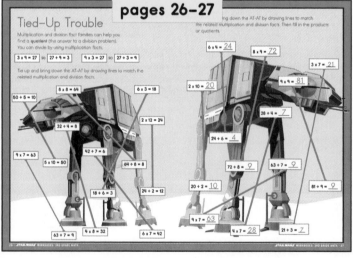

Tied-Up Trouble

Multiplication and division fact families can help you find a **quotient** (the answer to a division problem). You can divide by using multiplication facts.

$3 \times 9 = 27$ so $27 \div 9 = 3$ $9 \times 3 = 27$ so $27 \div 3 = 9$

Tie up and bring down the AT-AT by drawing lines to match the related multiplication and division facts.

$50 \div 5 = 10$
$8 \times 8 = 64$
$32 \div 4 = 8$
$5 \times 10 = 50$
$42 \div 7 = 6$
$18 \div 6 = 3$
$9 \times 7 = 63$
$63 \div 7 = 9$
$4 \times 8 = 32$
$6 \times 3 = 18$
$2 \times 12 = 24$
$64 \div 8 = 8$
$24 \div 2 = 12$
$6 \times 7 = 42$

... bring down the AT-AT by drawing lines to match the related multiplication and division facts. Then fill in the products or quotients.

$6 \times 4 = 24$
$8 \times 9 = 72$
$3 \times 7 = 21$
$9 \times 9 = 81$
$2 \times 10 = 20$
$28 \div 4 = 7$
$24 \div 6 = 4$
$72 \div 8 = 9$
$63 \div 7 = 9$
$20 \div 2 = 10$
$9 \times 7 = 63$
$4 \times 7 = 28$
$81 \div 9 = 9$
$21 \div 3 = 7$

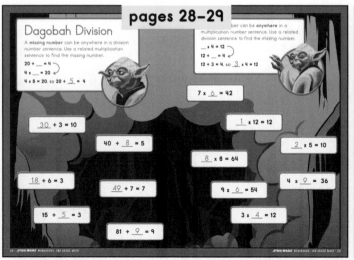

Dagobah Division

A **missing number** can be anywhere in a division number sentence. Use a related multiplication number sentence to find the missing number.
$20 \div \_ = 4$
$4 \times \_ = 20$
$4 \times 5 = 20$, so $20 \div 5 = 4$

A missing number can be anywhere in a multiplication number sentence. Use a related division sentence to find the missing number.
$\_ \times 4 = 12$
$12 \div \_ = 4$
$12 \div 4 = 3$, so $3 \times 4 = 12$

$30 \div 3 = 10$
$40 \div 8 = 5$
$18 \div 6 = 3$
$49 \div 7 = 7$
$15 \div 5 = 3$
$81 \div 9 = 9$

$7 \times 6 = 42$
$1 \times 12 = 12$
$2 \times 5 = 10$
$8 \times 8 = 64$
$9 \times 6 = 54$
$4 \times 9 = 36$
$3 \times 4 = 12$

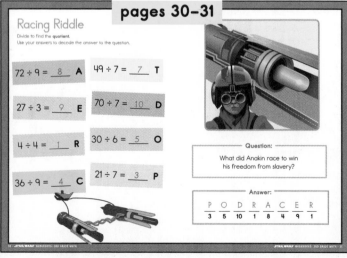

Racing Riddle

Divide to find the **quotient**. Use your answers to decode the answer to the question.

$72 \div 9 = 8$ **A**
$27 \div 3 = 9$ **E**
$4 \div 4 = 1$ **R**
$36 \div 9 = 4$ **C**

$49 \div 7 = 7$ **T**
$70 \div 7 = 10$ **D**
$30 \div 6 = 5$ **O**
$21 \div 7 = 3$ **P**

Question:
What did Anakin race to win his freedom from slavery?

Answer:

P	O	D	R	A	C	E	R
3	5	10	1	8	4	9	1

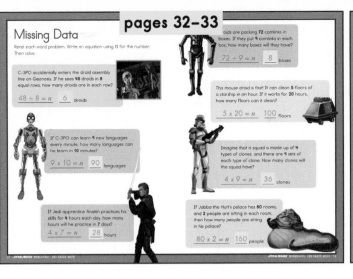

pages 32–33

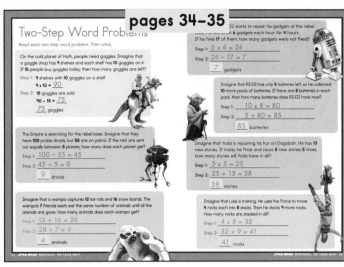

pages 34–35

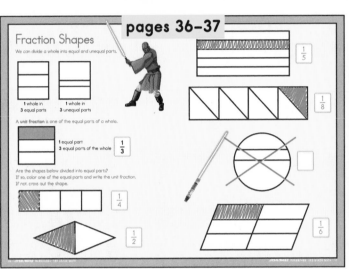

pages 36–37

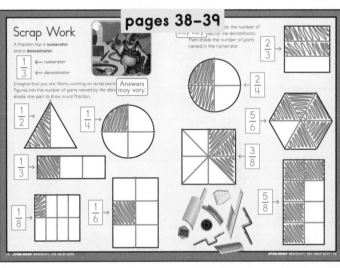

pages 38–39

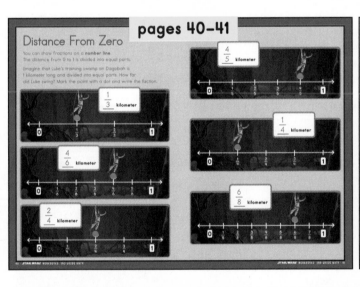

pages 40–41

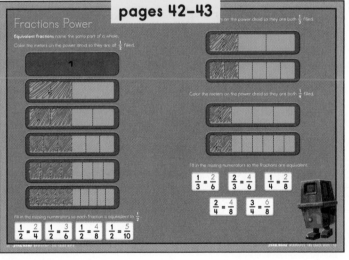

pages 42–43

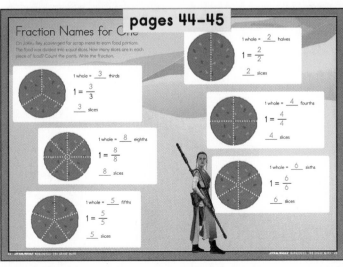

pages 44–45

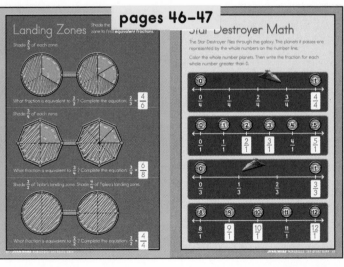

pages 46–47

Answers

pages 48–49

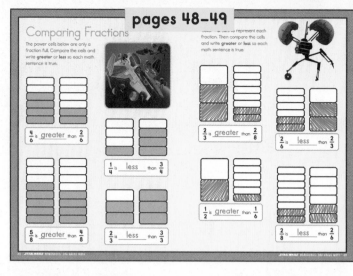

Comparing Fractions

The power cells below are only a fraction full. Compare the cells and write *greater* or *less* so each math sentence is true.

$\frac{4}{6}$ is __greater__ than $\frac{2}{6}$

$\frac{1}{4}$ is __less__ than $\frac{3}{4}$

$\frac{5}{8}$ is __greater__ than $\frac{4}{8}$

... to represent each fraction. Then compare the cells and write *greater* or *less* so each math sentence is true.

$\frac{2}{3}$ is __greater__ than $\frac{2}{8}$

$\frac{2}{3}$ is __less__ than $\frac{3}{3}$

$\frac{2}{6}$ is __less__ than $\frac{2}{3}$

$\frac{2}{8}$ is __less__ than $\frac{2}{6}$

pages 50–51

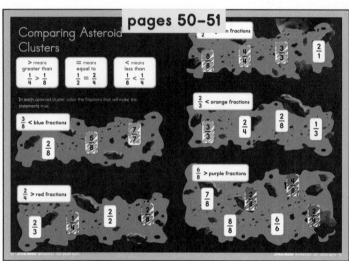

Comparing Asteroid Clusters

> means greater than $\frac{1}{4} > \frac{1}{8}$

= means equal to $\frac{1}{2} = \frac{2}{4}$

< means less than $\frac{1}{8} < \frac{1}{4}$

In each asteroid cluster, color the fractions that will make the statements true.

$\frac{3}{8}$ < blue fractions
$\frac{2}{8}$

$\frac{2}{4}$ > red fractions
$\frac{2}{3}$

... green fractions
$\frac{8}{8}$ $\frac{4}{4}$ $\frac{2}{1}$

$\frac{2}{4}$ < orange fractions
$\frac{3}{3}$ $\frac{2}{4}$ $\frac{1}{3}$

$\frac{6}{8}$ > purple fractions
$\frac{7}{8}$ $\frac{8}{8}$ $\frac{6}{6}$

pages 52–53

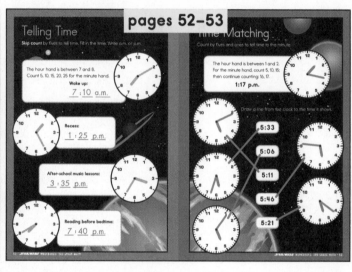

Telling Time

Skip count by fives to tell time. Fill in the time. Write a.m. or p.m.

The hour hand is between 7 and 8. Count 5, 10, 15, 20, 25 for the minute hand.

Wake up:
__7__ : __10__ a.m.

Recess:
__1__ : __25__ p.m.

After-school music lessons:
__3__ : __35__ p.m.

Reading before bedtime:
__7__ : __40__ p.m.

Time Matching

Count by fives and ones to tell time to the minute.

The hour hand is between 1 and 2. For the minute hand, count 5, 10, 15; then continue counting: 16, 17.

1:17 p.m.

Draw a line from the clock to the time it shows.

5:33
5:06
5:11
5:46
5:21

pages 54–55

Time Travels

Imagine that you are on a journey through the galaxy in the Millennium Falcon. Draw hands on the clocks to show the time you would arrive on each planet.

It is **7:46** when you arrive on Jakku.

It is **3:17** when you arrive on Hoth.

It is **11:12** when you arrive on Tatooine.

... you arrive on Naboo.

It is **12:33** when you arrive on Dagobah.

What time is it on your planet? Fill in the blanks and draw hands on the clock. Then draw a picture of your planet.

It is ___:___ on ___

pages 56–57

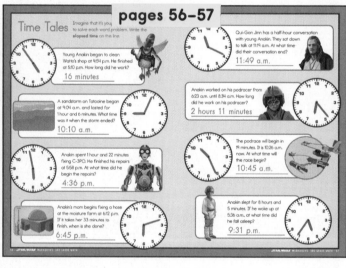

Time Tales

Imagine that it's your ... to solve each word problem. Write the **elapsed time** on the line.

Young Anakin began to clean Watto's shop at 4:54 p.m. He finished at 5:10 p.m. How long did he work?
16 minutes

A sandstorm on Tatooine began at 9:04 a.m. and lasted for 1 hour and 6 minutes. What time was it when the storm ended?
10:10 a.m.

Anakin spent 1 hour and 22 minutes fixing C-3PO. He finished his repairs at 5:58 p.m. At what time did he begin the repairs?
4:36 p.m.

Anakin's mom begins fixing a hose at the moisture farm at 6:12 p.m. If it takes her 33 minutes to finish, when is she done?
6:45 p.m.

Qui-Gon Jinn has a half-hour conversation with young Anakin. They sat down to talk at 11:19 a.m. At what time did their conversation end?
11:49 a.m.

Anakin worked on his podracer from 6:23 a.m. until 8:34 a.m. How long did he work on his podracer?
2 hours 11 minutes

The podrace will begin in 19 minutes. It is 10:26 a.m. now. At what time will the race begin?
10:45 a.m.

Anakin slept for 8 hours and 5 minutes. If he woke up at 5:36 a.m., at what time did he fall asleep?
9:31 p.m.

pages 58–59

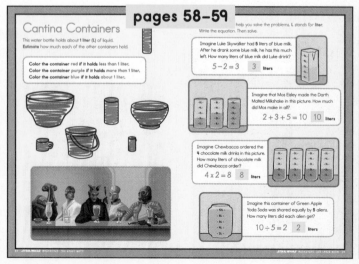

Cantina Containers

This water bottle holds about **1 liter (L)** of liquid. **Estimate** how much each of the other containers hold.

Color the container red if it holds less than 1 liter.
Color the container purple if it holds more than 1 liter.
Color the container blue if it holds about 1 liter.

... help you solve the problems. L stands for **liter**. Write the equation. Then solve.

Imagine Luke Skywalker had **5** liters of blue milk. After he drank some blue milk, he has this much left. How many liters of blue milk did Luke drink?
$5 - 2 = 3$ **3** liters

Imagine that Mos Eisley made the Darth Malted Milkshake in this picture. How much did Mos make in all?
$2 + 3 + 5 = 10$ **10** liters

Imagine Chewbacca ordered the **4** chocolate milk drinks in this picture. How many liters of chocolate milk did Chewbacca order?
$4 \times 2 = 8$ **8** liters

Imagine this container of Green Apple Yoda Soda was shared equally by **5** aliens. How many liters did each alien get?
$10 \div 5 = 2$ **2** liters

pages 60–61

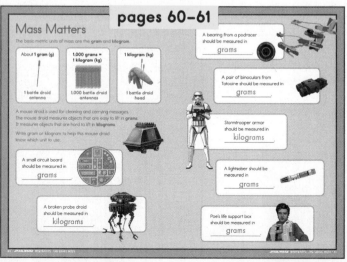

Mass Matters

The basic metric units of mass are the **gram** and **kilogram**.

About **1 gram (g)**
1 battle droid antenna

1,000 grams = 1 kilogram (kg)
1,000 battle droid antennas

1 kilogram (kg)
1 battle droid head

A mouse droid is used for cleaning and carrying messages. The mouse droid measures objects that are easy to lift in **grams**. It measures objects that are hard to lift in **kilograms**.

Write gram or kilogram to help this mouse droid know which unit to use.

A small circuit board should be measured in __grams__

A broken probe droid should be measured in __kilograms__

A bearing from a podracer should be measured in __grams__

A pair of binoculars from Tatooine should be measured in __grams__

Stormtrooper armor should be measured in __kilograms__

A lightsaber should be measured in __grams__

Poe's life support box should be measured in __grams__

pages 62–63

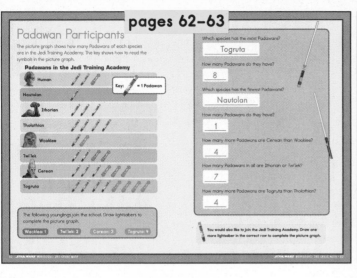

Padawan Participants

The picture graph shows how many Padawans of each species are in the Jedi Training Academy. The key shows how to read the symbols in the picture graph.

Padawans in the Jedi Training Academy
- Human
- Nautolan
- Ithorian
- Tholothian
- Wookiee
- Twi'lek
- Cerean
- Togruta

Key: = 1 Padawan

Which species has the most Padawans?
Togruta

How many Padawans do they have?
8

Which species has the fewest Padawans?
Nautolan

How many Padawans do they have?
1

How many more Padawans are Cerean than Wookiee?
4

How many Padawans in all are Ithorian or Twi'lek?
7

How many more Padawans are Togruta than Tholothian?
4

The following younglings join the school. Draw lightsabers to complete the picture graph.
Wookiee: 1 Twi'lek: 2 Cerean: 3 Togruta: 4

You would also like to join the Jedi Training Academy. Draw one more lightsaber in the correct row to complete the picture graph.

pages 64–65

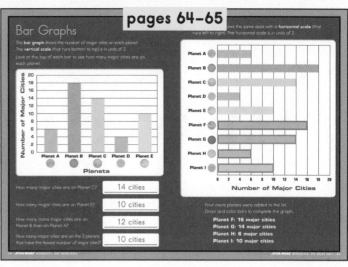

Bar Graphs

This bar graph shows the number of major cities on each planet. The vertical scale (that runs bottom to top) is in units of 2. Look at the top of each bar to see how many major cities are on each planet.

...ows the same data with a horizontal scale (that runs left to right). The horizontal scale is in units of 2.

How many major cities are on Planet C? **14 cities**

How many major cities are on Planet E? **10 cities**

How many more major cities are on Planet B than on Planet A? **12 cities**

How many major cities are on the 2 planets that have the fewest number of major cities? **10 cities**

Four more planets were added to the list. Draw and color bars to complete the graph.
- Planet F: 16 major cities
- Planet G: 14 major cities
- Planet H: 6 major cities
- Planet I: 10 major cities

pages 66–67

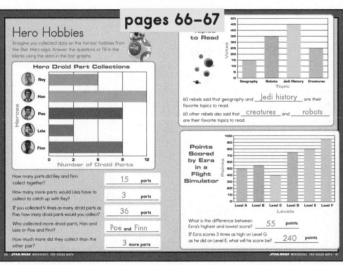

Hero Hobbies

Imagine you collected data on the heroes' hobbies from the *Star Wars* saga. Answer the questions or fill in the blanks using the data in the bar graphs.

Hero Droid Part Collections
Heroes: Rey, Han, Poe, Leia, Finn
Number of Droid Parts

How many parts did Rey and Finn collect together? **15 parts**

How many more parts would Leia have to collect to catch up with Rey? **3 parts**

If you collected 4 times as many droid parts as Poe, how many droid parts would you collect? **36 parts**

Who collected more droid parts, Han and Leia or Poe and Finn? **Poe and Finn**

How much more did they collect than the other pair? **3 more parts**

...Topic to Read

60 rebels said that geography and **Jedi history** are their favorite topics to read.

60 other rebels also said that **creatures** and **robots** are their favorite topics to read.

Points Scored by Ezra in a Flight Simulator
Levels

What is the difference between Ezra's highest and lowest score? **55 points**

If Ezra scores 3 times as high on Level G as he did on Level E, what will his score be? **240 points**

pages 68–69

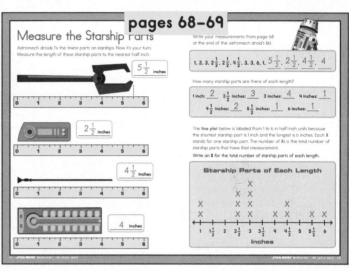

Measure the Starship Parts

Astromech droids fix the tiniest parts on starships. Now it's your turn. Measure the length of these starship parts to the nearest half inch.

$5\frac{1}{2}$ inches

$2\frac{1}{2}$ inches

$4\frac{1}{2}$ inches

4 inches

Write your measurements from page 68 at the end of the astromech droid's list.

1, 3, 3, $2\frac{1}{2}$, $2\frac{1}{2}$, $4\frac{1}{2}$, 3, 6, 1, $5\frac{1}{2}$, $2\frac{1}{2}$, $4\frac{1}{2}$, 4

How many starship parts are there of each length?

1 inch: **2** $2\frac{1}{2}$ inches: **3**   3 inches: **4**   4 inches: **1**
$4\frac{1}{2}$ inches: **2** $5\frac{1}{2}$ inches: **1**   6 inches: **1**

The line plot below is labeled from 1 to 6 in half-inch units because the shortest starship part is 1 inch and the longest is 6 inches. Each X stands for one starship part. The number of Xs is the total number of starship parts that have that measurement.

Write an X for the total number of starship parts of each length.

Starship Parts of Each Length
Inches (1, $1\frac{1}{2}$, 2, $2\frac{1}{2}$, 3, $3\frac{1}{2}$, 4, $4\frac{1}{2}$, 5, $5\frac{1}{2}$, 6)

pages 70–71

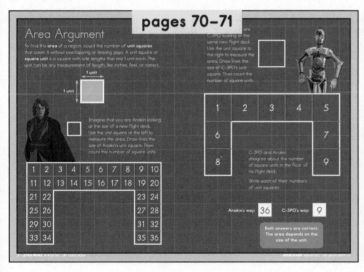

Area Argument

To find the area of a region, count the number of unit squares that cover it without overlapping or leaving gaps. A unit square or square unit is a square with side lengths that are 1 unit each. The unit can be any measurement of length, like inches, feet, or meters.

1 unit × 1 unit

Imagine that you are Anakin looking at the size of a new flight deck. Use the unit square at the left to measure the area. Draw lines the size of Anakin's unit square. Then count the number of square units.

...are C-3PO looking at the same new flight deck. Use the unit square to the right to measure the area. Draw lines the size of C-3PO's unit square. Then count the number of square units.

C-3PO and Anakin disagree about the number of square units in the floor of his flight deck. Write each of their numbers of unit squares.

Anakin's way: **36**   C-3PO's way: **9**

Both answers are correct. The area depends on the size of the unit.

pages 72–73

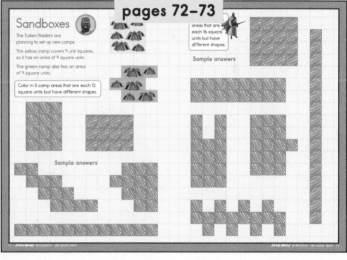

Sandboxes

The Tusken Raiders are planning to set up new camps.

This yellow camp covers 9 square units, so it has an area of 9 square units.

The green camp also has an area of 9 square units.

Color in 5 camp areas that are each 12 square units but have different shapes.

...areas that are each 16 square units but have different shapes.

Sample answers

pages 74–75

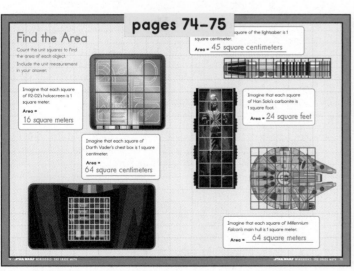

Find the Area

Count the unit squares to find the area of each object. Include the unit measurement in your answer.

...square of the lightsaber is 1 square centimeter.
Area = **45 square centimeters**

Imagine that each square of R2-D2's holoscreen is 1 square meter.
Area = **16 square meters**

Imagine that each square of Darth Vader's chest box is 1 square centimeter.
Area = **64 square centimeters**

Imagine that each square of Han Solo's carbonite is 1 square foot.
Area = **24 square feet**

Imagine that each square of *Millennium Falcon*'s main hull is 1 square meter.
Area = **64 square meters**

pages 76–77

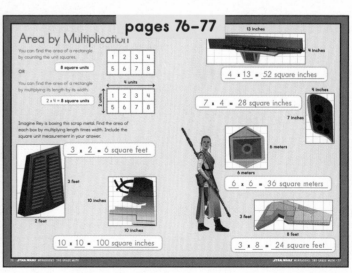

Area by Multiplication

You can find the area of a rectangle by counting the unit squares.
8 square units

OR

You can find the area of a rectangle by multiplying its length by its width.
$2 \times 4 = 8$ square units

Imagine Rey is boxing this scrap metal. Find the area of each box by multiplying length times width. Include the square unit measurement in your answer.

$3 \times 2 = 6$ square feet

$4 \times 13 = 52$ square inches

$7 \times 4 = 28$ square inches

$6 \times 6 = 36$ square meters

$10 \times 10 = 100$ square inches

$3 \times 8 = 24$ square feet

Answers

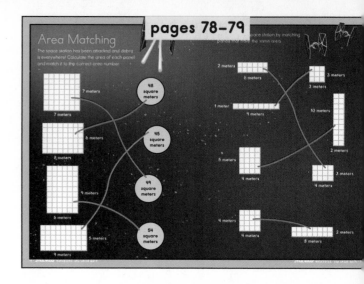

pages 78–79

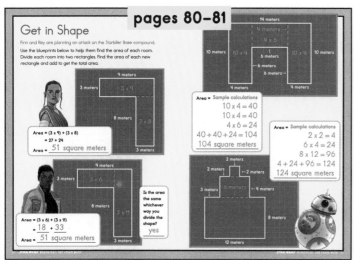

pages 80–81

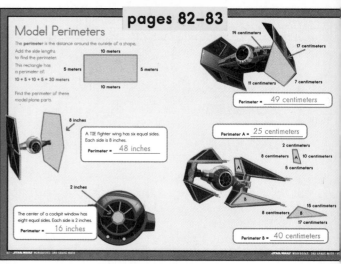

pages 82–83

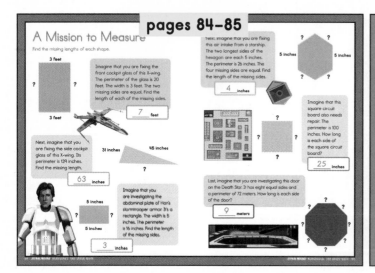

pages 84–85

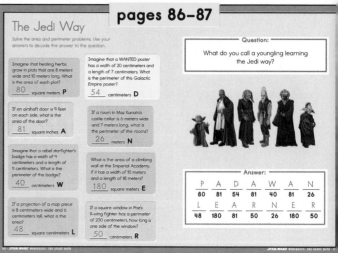

pages 86–87

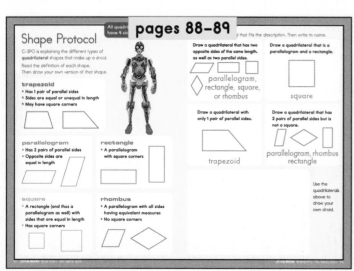

pages 88–89

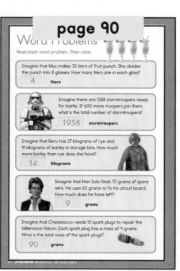

page 90